THE
WOOD
WORKING
HANDBOOK

THE WOOD WORKING HANDBOOK

TOM BEGNAL

BETTERWAY BOOKS
Cincinnati, Ohio

To prevent accidents, keep safety in mind while you work. Use the safety guards installed on power equipment; they are for your protection. When working on power equipment, keep fingers away from saw blades, wear safety goggles to prevent injuries from flying wood chips and sawdust, wear ear protection to protect your hearing, and consider installing a dust vacuum to reduce the amount of airborne sawdust in your woodshop. Don't wear loose clothing, such as neckties or shirts with loose sleeves, or jewelry, such as rings, necklaces or bracelets, when working on power equipment, and tie back long hair to prevent it from getting caught in your equipment. People who are sensitive to certain chemicals should check the chemical content of any product before using it. The author and editors who compiled this book have tried to make all the contents as accurate and correct as possible. Plans, illustrations, photographs and text have been carefully checked. All instructions, plans and projects should be carefully read, studied and understood before beginning construction. Due to the variability of local conditions, construction materials, skill levels, etc., neither the author nor Betterway Books assumes any responsibility for any accidents, injuries, damages or other losses incurred resulting from the material presented in this book.

A note about conversions: Conversion table for metric equivalents can be found on pages 25-29.

The Woodworking Handbook. Copyright © 1997 by Tom Begnal. Printed and bound in the United States of America. All rights reserved. No part of this book may be reproduced in any form or by any electronic or mechanical means including information storage and retrieval systems without permission in writing from the publisher, except by a reviewer, who may quote brief passages in a review. Published by Betterway Books, an imprint of F&W Publications, Inc., 1507 Dana Avenue, Cincinnati, Ohio 45207. (800) 289-0963. First edition.

This hardcover edition of *The Woodworking Handbook* features a "self-jacket" that eliminates the need for a separate dust jacket. It provides sturdy protection for your book while it saves paper, trees and energy.

Other fine Betterway Books are available from your local bookstore or direct from the publisher.

01 00 99 98 97   5 4 3 2 1

Library of Congress Cataloging-in-Publication Data

Begnal, Tom.
    The woodworking handbook / Tom Begnal.
        p.   cm.
    Includes index.
    ISBN 1-55870-463-9 (alk.paper)
    1. Woodwork. I. Title.
TT180.B425   1997
684'.08—dc21   97-11378
                                                                                 CIP

Edited by R. Adam Blake
Content edited by Bruce Stoker
Production edited by Amy Jeynes
Designed by Chad Planner

DEDICATION

To my wife Susan, for all her love and kindness

ACKNOWLEDGMENTS

I couldn't possibly have put together this book without considerable help. My grateful thanks and appreciation to the following individuals and organizations:

American Hardboard Association, Palatine, Illinois; American Wood Preservers Institute, Vienna, Virginia; Anchor Wire Corporation, Goodlettsville, Tennessee; APA—The Engineered Wood Association, Tacoma, Washington; Black and Decker, Hampstead, Maryland; Diamond Machining Technology, Marlborough, Massachusetts; Formica Corporation, Indianapolis, Indiana; Freud U.S.A., High Point, North Carolina; Hardwood Plywood and Veneer Association, Reston, Virginia; Hillman Fastener, Cincinnati, Ohio; Medite Corporation, Medford, Oregon; National Particleboard Association, Gaithersburg, Maryland; Norton Company, Worcester, Massachusetts; Dr. Mark Stephenson, National Institute for Occupational Safety and Health, Cincinnati, Ohio; The Olson Saw Company, Bethel, Connecticut; PPG Industries, Pittsburgh, Pennsylvania; United States Department of Agriculture, Washington, DC; Stephanie Dingler, Western Wood Products Association, Portland, Oregon; and Jody Garrett, Woodcraft Supply, Parkersburg, West Virginia.

Also, many thanks to Adam Blake, my editor at Betterway Books, who not only presented me with the book idea but also provided a good measure of help and encouragement along the way.

ABOUT THE AUTHOR

Tom Begnal was managing editor of *The Woodworker's Journal* magazine for more than fifteen years. He has written or edited woodworking and how-to books for several publishers including F&W Publications (Betterway Books), McGraw-Hill, Rodale Press and Sterling Publishing. He lives in Kent, Connecticut.

TOPIC INDEX

INTRODUCTION

As we enjoy an evening in the workshop, it is easy to forget that the craft of wood-working encompasses a surprisingly large body of information. Much of that information is learned only through considerable practice and experience. And, once learned, it is usually applied to the task at hand with little thought or effort. An experienced woodworker knows, almost intuitively, what to do and how to do it.

But, even veteran woodworkers understand that practice, experience and intuition are not always enough. Despite what seems to be second nature, it's often necessary to find an important bit of information in order to move a project forward. Usually, however, that bit of information is found only after a lengthy search through a pile of woodworking books, magazines, owner's manuals and shopworn notes. And, of course, the search too often comes up empty.

The Woodworking Handbook is an effort to make that search considerably easier. Here, in a single volume, is an easy-to-understand compilation of the many facts, figures and formulas that are important to every woodworker. From shop geometry to lumber grades to drill press speeds, *The Woodworking Handbook* provides an extensive storehouse of valuable woodworking data.

This is a book to be used, not admired. Keep it near your workbench. My sincere hope is that you often find yourself reaching for *The Woodworking Handbook*, and that it quickly provides you with all the information you need.

Have fun and work safely.

CHAPTER 1

WOODWORKING MATH

BASIC GEOMETRY FOR WOODWORKERS

An understanding of basic geometry is very useful to woodworkers. Indeed, when you consider that every woodworking project is made from parts that form straight lines, curved lines or a combination of the two, it is clear that geometry is very much a part of the workshop.

ANGLES

The space between two lines that meet is called an angle. An angle is usually measured in degrees.

Right Angle

The angle formed by a line perpendicular to another line. A right angle measures 90°.

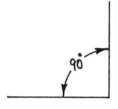

Acute Angle

An angle measuring less than a right angle.

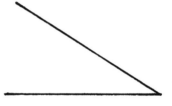

Obtuse Angle

An angle larger than a right angle, but less than 180°.

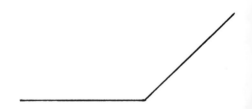

POLYGONS

A polygon is a closed plane figure that has three or more sides and angles. A polygon with all angles equal and all equal-length sides is called a regular polygon. Some of the common polygons are:

POLYGON	NUMBER OF SIDES	POLYGON	NUMBER OF SIDES
Triangle	3	Octagon	8
Quadrilateral	4	Decagon	10
Pentagon	5	Dodecagon	12
Hexagon	6		

TRIANGLES

A triangle is a polygon with three sides and three angles. The sum of the three angles is always 180°.

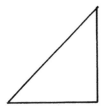

Right Triangle
A triangle with one angle at 90°.

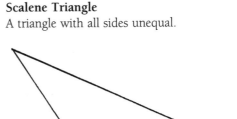

Scalene Triangle
A triangle with all sides unequal.

Equilateral Triangle
A triangle with all sides equal-length.

Isosceles Triangle
A triangle with two sides equal-length.

Obtuse Triangle
A triangle with one angle obtuse (greater than 90°).

QUADRILATERALS

A quadrilateral is a polygon that has four sides and four angles. The sum of the four angles is always 360°.

Rectangle
A four-sided plane figure with four right angles.

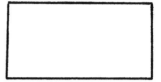

Square
A four-sided plane figure with four right angles and four equal-length sides.

Rhomboid
A four-sided plane figure with all sides parallel, adjacent sides unequal, and usually having two acute angles and two obtuse angles.

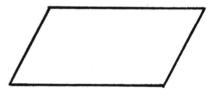

Rhombus
A four-sided plane figure with all sides equal-length and parallel, usually having two acute angles and two obtuse angles.

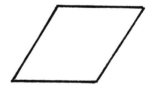

Trapezoid
A four-sided plane figure with two sides parallel and two sides not parallel.

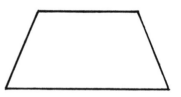

Trapezium
A four-sided plane figure having no sides parallel.

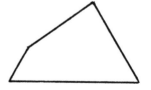

OTHER POLYGONS

Regular Pentagon
A plane figure having five equal-length sides and five equal angles.

Regular Hexagon
A plane figure having six equal-length sides and six equal angles.

Regular Octagon
A plane figure having eight equal-length sides and eight equal angles.

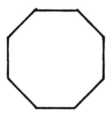

Regular Decagon
A plane figure having ten equal-length sides and ten equal angles.

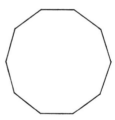

Regular Dodecagon
A plane figure having twelve equal-length sides and twelve equal angles.

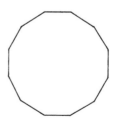

CIRCLES

A circle is a closed curve, with all points on the curve equally distant from the center.

Radius
A straight line extending from the center of the circle to any point on the circle.

Diameter
A straight line that passes through the center of a circle and extends from one side of the circle to the other.

Chord
A straight line connecting two points on a circle.

Tangent
A straight line that touches a circle at only one point.

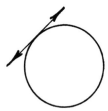

Segment
That part of a circle cut off by a straight line.

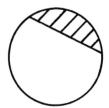

AREA FORMULAS

Area is a measure of the amount of surface of an object. Square units of measurement (square inches, square feet, square millimeters, square meters, etc.) are used to describe area.

Triangle

Area = ½B × H

where:

B = length of the triangle base

H = height of the triangle

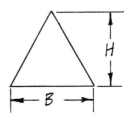

Example

B = 12″   H = 8″

Area = ½(12) × 8

= 6 × 8

= 48 square inches

Square

Area = S × S

where:

S = length of the sides

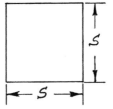

Example

S = 6″

Area = 6 × 6

= 36 square inches

Rectangle

Area = L × W

where:

L = length of the rectangle

W = width of the rectangle

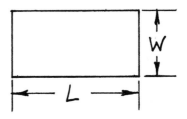

Example

L = 4″   W = 2″

Area = 4 × 2

= 8 square inches

Trapezoid

Area = ½(L1 + L2) × W

where:

L1 = long parallel side

L2 = short parallel side

W = width of trapezoid

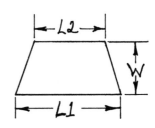

Example

L1 = 12″   L2 = 8″

W = 5″

Area = ½(12 + 8) × 5

= ½(20) × 5

= 10 × 5

= 50 square inches

Trapezium

Area = $[(G+H)E + (F \times G) + (D \times H)]/2$

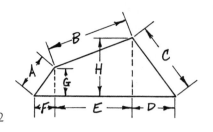

Example

A = 5″	B = 11.75″
C = 10″	D = 6″
E = 11″	F = 3″
G = 4″	H = 8″

Area = $[(4+8)11 + (3 \times 4) + (6 \times 8)]/2$

$= [(12)11 + 12 + 48]/2$

$= [132 + 12 + 48]/2$

$= 192/2$

$= 96$ square inches

Regular Pentagon
(all sides equal)

Area = $1.7205 \times (A \times A)$

where:

A = length of sides

Example

A = 6″

Area = $1.7205 \times (6 \times 6)$

$= 1.7205 \times 36$

$= 61.938$ square inches

Regular Hexagon
(all sides equal)

Area = $2.5981 \times (A \times A)$

where:

A = length of sides

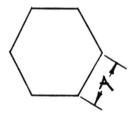

Example

A = 2″

Area = $2.5981 \times (2 \times 2)$

$= 2.5981 \times 4$

$= 10.3924$ square inches

Regular Octagon
(all sides equal)

Area = $4.8284 \times (A \times A)$

where:

A = length of sides

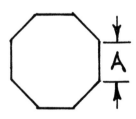

Example

A = 3″

Area = $4.8284 \times (3 \times 3)$

$= 4.8284 \times 9$

$= 43.456$ square inches

Circle

Area $= 3.14159 \times (R \times R)$

where:

R = radius of circle

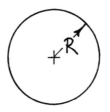

Example

R = 15″

Area $= 3.14159 \times (15 \times 15)$

$= 3.14159 \times 225$

$= 706.86$ square inches

WOODSHOP APPLICATION

Using the Area Formula

Two coats of polyurethane varnish must be applied to the top and bottom surfaces of a round tabletop that has a 48″ diameter. Is a pint of polyurethane enough to do the job?

1. Determine the area of the tabletop surface in square inches. 48″ diameter means 24″ radius.

    Area $= 3.14159 \times (R \times R)$

    $= 3.14159 \times (24 \times 24)$

    $= 3.14159 \times 576$

    $= 1810$ square inches

    Multiply by 2 to get area for the top and bottom surfaces.

    $1810 \times 2 = 3620$ square inches.

2. Convert square inches to square feet (see conversion table on page 29).

    3620 square inches $\times$ .00694 $= 25.12$ square feet. Multiply by 2 to get amount needed for two coats.

    $25.12 \times 2 = 50.24$ square feet.

3. Check label on can for coverage of product.

A pint of polyurethane that can cover at least 60 square feet will be able to do the job.

PERIMETER FORMULAS

Perimeter is the distance around the outside of a geometric figure.

Triangle

Perimeter = A + B + C

where:

A, B and C = lengths of sides

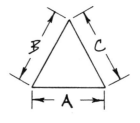

Example

A = 5"   C = 12"

B = 8"

Perimeter = 5 + 8 + 12

= 25"

Square

Perimeter = 4 × S

where:

S = length of sides

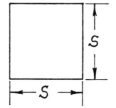

Example

S = 9"

Perimeter = 4 × 9

= 36"

Rectangle

Perimeter = 2 × (L + W)

where:

L = length of the rectangle

W = width of the rectangle

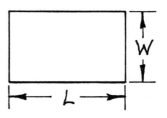

Example

L = 6.5"   W = 3.5"

Perimeter = 2 × (6.5 + 3.5)

= 2 × 10

= 20"

Trapezoid

Perimeter = A + B + C + D

where:

A, B, C and D = lengths of sides

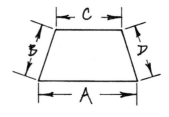

Example

A = 5"   C = 4"

B = 8"   D = 6"

Perimeter = 5 + 8 + 4 + 6

= 23"

Trapezium
Perimeter $= A + B + C + D$
where:
A, B, C and D $=$ lengths of sides
Example
$A = 18.25''$ $C = 6.25''$
$B = 5.5''$ $D = 8''$
Perimeter $= 18.25 + 5.5 + 6.25 + 8$
$= 38''$

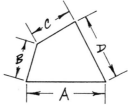

Other Regular Polygons
(hexagon is shown)
Perimeter $= A \times N$
where:
A $=$ length of sides
N $=$ number of sides
Example
$A = 4''$
N (for hexagon) $= 6$
Perimeter $= 4 \times 6$
$= 24''$

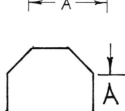

WOODSHOP APPLICATION

Using the Perimeter Formula
A cove molding is to be added around the base of a blanket chest. The blanket chest measures 18″ wide by 48″ long. How much cove molding must be routed in order to provide enough stock for the project?

1. Determine the perimeter of the rectangular blanket chest.
   Perimeter $= 2 (A + B)$
   $= 2 (18 + 48)$
   $= 2 (66)$
   $= 132''$

2. Convert inches to feet (see conversion table on page 27).
   $132'' \times .08333 = 11'$

The blanket chest needs a minimum of 11′ of routed molding.

CIRCUMFERENCE FORMULA

The circumference is the distance around a circle.

Circle
Circumference = 6.2832 × R
where:
R = radius of circle
> **Example**
> R = 12″
> Circumference = 6.2832 × 12
>   = 75.4″

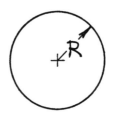

WOODSHOP APPLICATION

Using the Circumference Formula
How much iron-on edging is required in order to apply the edging to a 36″ diameter tabletop?

1. Determine the radius of the tabletop.
   Radius = Diameter/2
          = 36/2
          = 18″

2. Determine the circumference of the tabletop.
   Circumference = 6.2832 × R
                 = 6.2832 × 18
                 = 113″

3. Convert inches to feet (see conversion table on page 27).
   113″ × .08333 = 9.42′

The tabletop needs 10′ of iron-on edging.

SOLVING RIGHT TRIANGLES

Right triangles (triangles with one angle at 90°) are found in many woodworking designs, so the ability to solve these triangles is very helpful when designing or building many types of projects. Solving a right triangle enables you to determine the angles and the lengths of the sides.

Using the formulas that follow, you can determine the unknown *sides* of a right triangle if you know one of the angles (other than the 90° angle) and the length of one side. You can also determine the unknown *angles* of a right triangle if you know the length of at least two of the sides.

In some cases it might be necessary to use two of the formulas to get the answer you need. The first formula solves for an unknown side or angle. Then, the new information is applied to a second formula that can provide the final answer.

Keep in mind that when the location of the unknown angle (A) changes, the location of sides B and C also changes as shown below.

Finally, remember that the three angles in a triangle always equal 180°. If you know one of the angles (other than the 90° angle) you can get the unknown angle using the formula: $180 - (90 + \text{known angle})$.

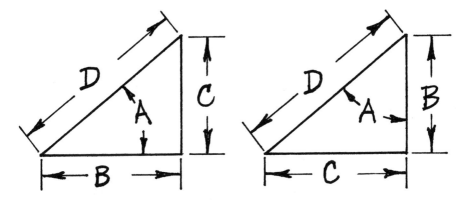

A = unknown angle (based on Angle Functions in Table I, II, or III on page 14)

B = side adjacent to the unknown angle

C = side opposite the unknown angle

D = side opposite the 90° angle

ANGLE (A) (degrees)	TABLE I	TABLE II	TABLE III
0	.00000	1.00000	.00000
1	.01746	.99985	.01745
2	.03492	.99939	.03490
3	.05241	.99863	.05234
4	.06993	.99756	.06976
5	.08749	.99619	.08716
6	.10510	.99452	.10453
7	.12278	.99255	.12187
8	.14054	.99027	.13937
9	.15838	.98769	.15643
10	.17633	.98481	.17365
11	.19438	.98163	.19081
12	.21256	.97815	.20791
13	.23087	.97437	.22495
14	.24933	.97030	.24192
15	.26795	.96593	.25882
16	.28675	.96126	.27564
17	.30573	.95630	.29237
18	.32492	.95106	.30902
19	.34433	.94552	.32557
20	.36397	.93969	.34202
21	.38386	.93358	.35837
22	.40403	.92718	.37461
23	.42447	.92050	.39073
24	.44523	.91355	.40674
25	.46631	.90631	.42262
26	.48773	.89879	.43837
27	.50953	.89101	.45399
28	.53171	.88295	.46947
29	.55431	.87462	.48481
30	.57735	.86603	.50000
31	.60086	.85717	.51504
32	.62487	.84805	.52992
33	.64941	.83867	.54464
34	.67451	.82904	.55919
35	.70021	.81915	.57358
36	.72654	.80902	.58779
37	.75355	.79864	.60182
38	.78129	.78801	.61566
39	.80978	.77715	.62932
40	.83910	.76604	.64279
41	.86929	.75471	.65606
42	.90040	.74314	.66913
43	.93252	.73135	.68200
44	.96569	.71934	.69466
45	1.0000	.70711	.70711

Solving Right Triangles When One Side and One Angle Are Known

If you know the length of:	And you want to know the length of:	Refer to pages 13–14 and use this formula:
B	C	C = A (from Table I) × B
B	D	D = B/A (from Table II)
C	B	B = C/A (from Table I)
C	D	D = C/A (from Table III)
D	C	C = A (from Table III) × D
D	B	B = A (from Table II) × D

WOODSHOP APPLICATION

A lap desk to be built must have sides that are 14″ long and have a 15° slant. If the front end of the sides measures 3″, what is the overall width of the sides?

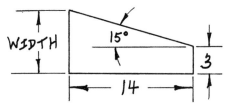

The desk side creates a right triangle with one known side (B) and one known angle (A). To determine the overall width of a side, calculate the length of side C, then add that length to 3″.

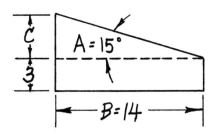

A = 15°
B = 14″
C = unknown

From the formulas above:
C = A (from Table I) × B
= .26795 × 14
= 3.7513 (round to 3.75 = 3¾″)
Width of sides = 3¾″ + 3″
= 6¾″

Solving Right Triangles When Two Sides Are Known

If you know the length of:	And you know the length of:	Refer to pages 13–14 and use this formula to find angle A:
B	C	A (from Table I) = C/B
B	D	A (from Table II) = B/D
C	D	A (from Table III) = C/D

Once the angle function (A) is determined, convert the number to the corresponding angle.

WOODSHOP APPLICATION

A coffee table is to have four 15″ long legs made from 1¾″ square stock. The legs are to be tapered on two sides, with each taper starting 4¼″ from the top of the leg. At the bottom of the leg, the taper reduces the thickness of the leg by ¾″. You need to determine the angle of the taper so you can use a tapering jig to cut the tapers.

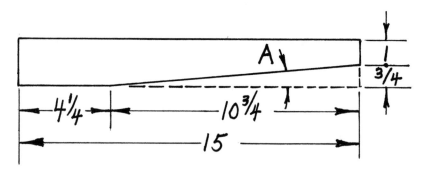

A = unknown
B = 10¾
C = .75

A (from Table I) = C/B
    = .75/10.75
    = .06977
From Table I: .06977 = about 4°

HOW TO DRAW AN ELLIPSE

Various methods can be used to create an ellipse. The method shown here, often called the trammel method, is relatively simple and can be used to make an ellipse of just about any size.

1. Draw a horizontal line slightly longer than the length of the ellipse, then draw a vertical line slightly longer than the ellipse width. Make sure the lines are perpendicular to each other.

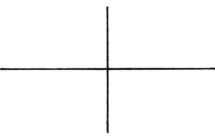

2. Mark points X, Y and Z on a straightedge made from cardboard, stiff paper or a thin piece of wood. XZ should be equal to one-half the length of the ellipse and XY should be equal to one-half the width of the ellipse.

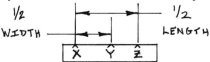

3. Position the straightedge so that point Z falls along the vertical line and point Y falls along the horizontal line. Hold the straightedge in position, then mark point X which represents a point on the circumference of the ellipse.

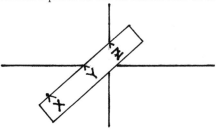

4. Continue moving the straightedge, always keeping point Z on the vertical line and point Y on the horizontal line. Mark a new point X after each movement of the straightedge. Mark as many points as needed to create a smooth curve along the entire circumference of the ellipse.

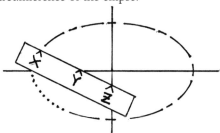

Drawing an Ellipse

Draw an elliptical tabletop that measures 48″ long by 30″ wide.

1. Draw a horizontal line at least 48″ long on the glued-up stock for the tabletop. At the midpoint of the horizontal line, draw a vertical line at least 30″ long. Make sure the lines are perpendicular to each other.

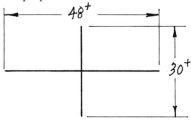

2. Mark points X, Y and Z, using a straightedge, so that XZ equals 24″ and XY equals 15″.

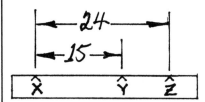

3. Position the straightedge so that point Z falls along the vertical line and point Y falls along the horizontal line. Hold the straightedge in position, then mark point X which represents a point on the circumference of the ellipse.

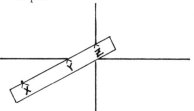

4. Continue moving the straightedge, always keeping point Z on the vertical line and point Y on the horizontal line. Mark point X after each movement of the straightedge. Mark as many points as needed to create a smooth curve along the entire circumference of the ellipse.

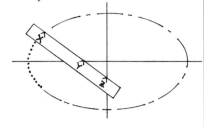

FRACTIONS TO DECIMAL EQUIVALENTS

FRACTION (inches)	DECIMAL EQUIVALENT (inches)	FRACTION (inches)	DECIMAL EQUIVALENT (inches)
$1/64$	.015625	$33/64$	.515625
$1/32$	.031250	$17/32$	.531250
$3/64$	.046875	$35/64$	.546875
$1/16$	.062500	$9/16$	.562500
$5/64$	.078125	$37/64$	.578125
$3/32$	.093750	$19/32$	.593750
$7/64$	.109375	$39/64$	.609375
$1/8$	.125000	$5/8$	.625000
$9/64$	.140625	$41/64$	.640625
$5/32$	.156250	$21/32$	.656250
$11/64$	.171875	$43/64$	.671875
$3/16$	.187500	$11/16$	.687500
$13/64$	.203125	$45/64$	.703125
$7/32$	.218750	$23/32$	.718750
$15/64$	.234375	$47/64$	.734375
$1/4$	.250000	$3/4$	.750000
$17/64$	.265625	$49/64$	.765625
$9/32$	.281250	$25/32$	.781250
$19/64$	.296875	$51/64$	.796875
$5/16$	.312500	$13/16$	.812500
$21/64$	.328125	$53/64$	.828125
$11/32$	.343750	$27/32$	.843750
$23/64$	.359375	$55/64$	.859375
$3/8$	.375000	$7/8$	.875000
$25/64$	.390625	$57/64$	.890625
$13/32$	.406250	$29/32$	.906250
$27/64$	.421875	$59/64$	.921875
$7/16$	.437500	$15/16$	.937500
$29/64$	.453125	$61/64$	.953125
$15/32$	.468750	$31/32$	.968750
$31/64$	.484375	$63/64$	.984375
$1/2$	.500000	1	1.00000

FRACTIONS TO METRIC EQUIVALENTS

FRACTION (inches)	METRIC EQUIVALENT (millimeters)	FRACTION (inches)	METRIC EQUIVALENT (millimeters)
$1/64$	0.396875	$33/64$	13.09688
$1/32$	0.793750	$17/32$	13.49375
$3/64$	1.190625	$35/64$	13.89063
$1/16$	1.587500	$9/16$	14.28750
$5/64$	1.984375	$37/64$	14.68438
$3/32$	2.381250	$19/32$	15.08125
$7/64$	2.778125	$39/64$	15.47813
$1/8$	3.175000	$5/8$	15.87500
$9/64$	3.571875	$41/64$	16.27188
$5/32$	3.968750	$21/32$	16.66875
$11/64$	4.365625	$43/64$	17.06563
$3/16$	4.762500	$11/16$	17.46250
$13/64$	5.159375	$45/64$	17.85938
$7/32$	5.556250	$23/32$	18.25625
$15/64$	5.953125	$47/64$	18.65313
$1/4$	6.350000	$3/4$	19.05000
$17/64$	6.746875	$49/64$	19.44688
$9/32$	7.143750	$25/32$	19.84375
$19/64$	7.540625	$51/64$	20.24063
$5/16$	7.937500	$13/16$	20.63750
$21/64$	8.334375	$53/64$	21.03438
$11/32$	8.731250	$27/32$	21.43125
$23/64$	9.128125	$55/64$	21.82813
$3/8$	9.525000	$7/8$	22.22500
$25/64$	9.921875	$57/64$	22.62188
$13/32$	10.31875	$29/32$	23.01875
$27/64$	10.71563	$59/64$	23.41563
$7/16$	11.11250	$15/16$	23.81250
$29/64$	11.50938	$61/64$	24.20938
$15/32$	11.90625	$31/32$	24.60625
$31/64$	12.30313	$63/64$	25.00313
$1/2$	12.70000	1	25.40000

METRIC TO DECIMAL EQUIVALENTS

METRIC (millimeters)	DECIMAL EQUIVALENT (inches)
1	.03937
2	.07874
3	.11811
4	.15748
5	.19685
6	.23622
7	.27559
8	.31496
9	.35433
10	.39370
11	.43307
12	.47244
13	.51181
14	.55118
15	.59055
16	.62992
17	.66929
18	.70866
19	.74803
20	.78740
21	.82677
22	.86614
23	.90551
24	.94488
25	.98425
26	1.02362

U.S. WEIGHTS AND MEASURES

LENGTH

1 mil = .001 inch
1000 mils = 1 inch = .08333 foot
12 inches = 1 foot = .33333 yard
3 feet = 1 yard = 36 inches
5½ yards = 1 rod = 16½ feet

SQUARE MEASURE (AREA)

1 square inch = .00694 square foot = .00077 square yard
144 square inches = 1 square foot = .11111 square yard
9 square feet = 1 square yard = 1296 square inches
30¼ square yards = 1 square rod = .00625 acre

CUBIC MEASURE (VOLUME)

1 cubic inch = .00058 cubic foot = .00002 cubic yard
1728 cubic inches = 1 cubic foot = .0370 cubic yard
27 cubic feet = 1 cubic yard = 46,656 cubic inches
128 cubic feet = 1 cord = 4.736 cubic yards

CAPACITY—LIQUID MEASURE

60 minims = 1 fluidram = .22559 cubic inch
8 fluidrams = 1 fluid ounce = 1.80469 cubic inches
4 fluid ounces = 1 gill = 7.21875 cubic inches
4 gills = 1 pint = 28.875 cubic inches
2 pints = 1 quart = 57.75 cubic inches
4 quarts = 1 gallon = 231 cubic inches
31½ gallons = 1 barrel = 7277 cubic inches

CAPACITY—DRY MEASURE

1 pint = ½ quart = 33.6 cubic inches
2 pints = 1 quart = 67.2 cubic inches
8 quarts = 1 peck = 537.6 cubic inches
4 pecks = 1 bushel = 2150 cubic inches

WEIGHT (AVOIRDUPOIS)

27.344 grains = 1 dram = .0625 ounce
16 drams = 1 ounce = 437.5 grains
16 ounces = 1 pound = 7000 grains
25 pounds = 1 quarter = 400 ounces
100 pounds = 1 short hundredweight = .05 short ton
112 pounds = 1 long hundredweight = .05 long ton
20 short hundredweight = 1 short ton = 2000 pounds
20 long hundredweight = 1 long ton = 2240 pounds

METRIC WEIGHTS AND MEASURES

LENGTH
1 millimeter = .001 meter
10 millimeters = 1 centimeter = .01 meter
10 centimeters = 1 decimeter = .10 meter
10 decimeters = 1 meter = 1 meter
10 meters = 1 dekameter = 10 meters
10 dekameters = 1 hectometer = 100 meters
10 hectometers = 1 kilometer = 1000 meters

SQUARE MEASURE (AREA)
100 square millimeters = 1 square centimeter = .0001 square meter
100 square centimeters = 1 square decimeter = .01 square meter
100 square decimeters = 1 square meter = 1 square meter
100 square meters = 1 square dekameter = 100 square meters
100 square dekameters = 1 square hectometer = 10,000 square meters

CUBIC MEASURE (VOLUME)
1000 cubic millimeters = 1 cubic centimeter = .000001 cubic meter
1000 cubic centimeters = 1 cubic decimeter = .001 cubic meter
1000 cubic decimeters = 1 cubic meter = 1 cubic meter

CAPACITY
10 milliliters = 1 centiliter = .01 liter
10 centiliters = 1 deciliter = .10 liter
10 deciliters = 1 liter = 1 liter
10 liters = 1 dekaliter = 10 liters
10 dekaliters = 1 hectoliter = 100 liters
10 hectoliters = 1 kiloliter = 1000 liters

WEIGHT
10 milligrams = 1 centigram = .01 gram
10 centigrams = 1 decigram = .10 gram
10 decigrams = 1 gram = 1 gram
10 grams = 1 dekagram = 10 grams
10 dekagrams = 1 hectogram = 100 grams
10 hectograms = 1 kilogram = 1000 grams
100 kilograms = 1 quintal = 100,000 grams
10 quintals = 1 ton = 1,000,000 grams

U.S. AND METRIC EQUIVALENTS

LENGTH

1 inch = 25.4 millimeters = 2.54 centimeters = .0254 meter
1 foot = 304.80 millimeters = 30.48 centimeters = .3048 meter
1 yard = 914.40 millimeters = 91.44 centimeters = .9144 meter

1 millimeter = .03937 inch = .00328083 foot = .00109361 yard
1 centimeter = .39370 inch = .03280830 foot = .01093610 yard
1 meter = 39.37 inches = 3.28083 feet = 1.093611 yards

SQUARE MEASURE (AREA)

1 square inch = 645.16 square millimeters = 6.4516 square centimeters = .00064516 square meter
1 square foot = 92,903 square millimeters = 929.03 square centimeters = .092903 square meter
1 square yard = 836,127 square millimeters = 8361.27 square centimeters = .836127 square meter

1 square millimeter = .0015499 square inch
1 square centimeter = .154999 square inch = .001076 square foot
1 square meter = 1549.99 square inches = 10.7638 square feet = 1.19599 square yards

CUBIC MEASURE (VOLUME)

1 cubic inch = 16,387 cubic millimeters = 16.3871 cubic centimeters
1 cubic foot = 28,317 cubic centimeters = .0283168 cubic meter
1 cubic yard = .7645548 cubic meter

1 cubic millimeter = .000061 cubic inch
1 cubic centimeter = .06102 cubic inch
1 cubic meter = 35.314 cubic feet = 1.3079 cubic yards

CAPACITY

1 minim = .061610 milliliter = .0000616 liter
1 fluidram = 3.6967 milliliters = .0036967 liter
1 fluid ounce = 29.5729 milliliters = .0295729 liter
1 gill = 118.294 milliliters = .118294 liter
1 pint (liquid) = 473.176 milliliters = .473176 liter
1 quart (liquid) = 946.35 milliliters = .94635 liter

1 gallon (liquid) = 3785.4 milliliters = 3.7854 liters
1 milliliter = .27 fluidram = .06102 cubic inch
1 centiliter = .338 fluid ounce = .61020 cubic inch
1 deciliter = .21 pint (liquid) = 6.1020 cubic inches
1 liter = 1.057 quarts (liquid) = 61.020 cubic inches
1 dekaliter = 2.64 gallons (liquid) = 244.080 cubic inches

WEIGHT

1 grain = .0648 gram
1 dram (avoirdupois) = 1.77185 grams
1 ounce (avoirdupois) = 28.3495 grams
1 pound (avoirdupois) = .4536 kilogram

1 short hundredweight = 45.359 kilograms
1 long hundredweight = 50.848 kilograms
1 short ton = .90718 metric ton
1 long ton = 1.0161 metric tons

CONVERSION TABLE

Note: British imperial measure (liquid and dry measure) is not shown. The British imperial gallon equals 1.2009 U.S. gallons.

TO CONVERT FROM:	TO:	MULTIPLY BY:
centigrams	grains	.15432
	grams	.01
centiliters	drams	2.705
	fluid ounces	.033814
	liters	.01
centimeters	feet	.03281
	inches	.3937
	meters	.01
	mils	393.7
cubic centimeters	cubic feet	.00003532
	cubic inches	.06102
	liters	.001
	cubic meters	.000001
cubic decimeters	cubic centimeters	1000
	cubic inches	61.0237
cubic feet	cubic centimeters	28,317
	cubic inches	1728
	cubic yards	.03704
	cubic meters	.02832
	gallons (liquid)	7.48052
	liters	28.31687
cubic inches	cubic centimeters	16.3872
	cubic feet	.000579
	cubic meters	.00001639
	gallons (liquid)	.00433
	liters	.01639
	pints (dry)	.02976
	pints (liquid)	.03463
	quarts (dry)	.01488
	quarts (liquid)	.01732
cubic meters	cubic centimeters	1,000,000
	cubic feet	35.314
	cubic inches	61,023.4
	gallons (liquid)	264.17
cubic millimeters	cubic centimeters	.001
	cubic inches	.00006

TO CONVERT FROM:	TO:	MULTIPLY BY:
cubic yards	cubic feet	27
	cubic inches	46,656
	cubic meters	.7646
decigrams	grains	1.5432
	grams	.1
deciliters	fluid ounces	.338
	liters	.1
decimeters	inches	3.937
	meters	.01
dekagrams	grams	10
	ounces (avoirdupois)	.3527
dekaliters	gallons (liquid)	2.64
	liters	10
dekameters	inches	393.7
	meters	10
drams (avoirdupois)	ounces (avoirdupois)	.0625
	grains	27.3437
	grams	1.7718
drams (liquid)	see fluidrams	
feet	centimeters	30.4801
	inches	12
	meters	.3048
	yards	.3333
fluid ounces	cubic inches	1.80469
	fluidrams	8.0
	gallons (liquid)	.00781
	liters	.02959
fluidrams	cubic inches	.22559
	fluid ounces	.125
	milliliters	3.69669
	minims	60
gallons (dry)	cubic feet	.1556
	cubic inches	268.8
	cubic meters	.004
gallons (liquid)	cubic feet	.1337
	cubic inches	231
	cubic meters	.0038
	fluid ounces	128
	liters	3.7854

TO CONVERT FROM:	TO:	MULTIPLY BY:
gills	pints (liquid)	.25
grains	drams (avoirdupois)	.03657
	grams	.0648
	milligrams	64.7989
	ounces (avoirdupois)	.00229
	pounds (avoirdupois)	.00014
grams	grains	15.432
	kilograms	.001
	milligrams	1000
	ounces (avoirdupois)	.03527
	pounds (avoirdupois)	.0022
hectograms	grams	100
	ounces (avoirdupois)	3.5274
hectoliters	gallons (liquid)	26.418
	liters	100
inches	centimeters	2.54
	feet	.08333
	meters	.0254
	mils	1000
	yards	.02778
kilograms	grains	15,432.36
	grams	1000
	ounces (avoirdupois)	35.274
	pounds (avoirdupois)	2.2046
kiloliters	gallons (liquid)	264.172
	liters	1000
kilometers	feet	3280.833
	meters	1000
liters	cubic centimeters	1000
	cubic feet	.035313
	cubic inches	61.02398
	quarts (dry)	.9081
	quarts (liquid)	1.0567
	gallons (dry)	.22702
	gallons (liquid)	.26417
long tons	pounds (avoirdupois)	2240
meters	feet	3.2808
	inches	39.37
	kilometers	.001
	millimeters	1000

CONVERSION TABLE (CONT'D)

TO CONVERT FROM:	TO:	MULTIPLY BY:
microns	inches	.0000394
	meters	.000001
	mils	.03937
milligrams	grains	.01543
	grams	.001
milliliters	fluid ounces	.0338
	fluidrams	.2705
	liters	.001
millimeters	inches	.03937
	meters	.001
	microns	1000
	mils	39.37
mils	inches	.001
	microns	25.4001
	millimeters	.0254
minims	fluidrams	.01667
	milliliters	.06161
ounces (avoirdupois)	drams (avoirdupois)	16
	grains	437.5
	grams	28.350
	pounds (avoirdupois)	.0625
ounces (liquid)	see fluid ounces	
pints (dry)	cubic inches	33.6003
	liters	.5506
	quarts (dry)	.5
pints (liquid)	cubic inches	28.875
	gills	4
	liters	.47318
pounds (avoirdupois)	grams	453.592
	grains	7000
	ounces (avoirdupois)	16
quarts (dry)	cubic inches	67.2006
	liters	1.10112
	pints (dry)	2
quarts (liquid)	cubic inches	57.75
	liters	.94636
	pints (liquid)	2
square centimeters	square feet	.001076
	square inches	.1550
	square millimeters	100

TO CONVERT FROM:	TO:	MULTIPLY BY:
square decimeters	square inches	15.5
	square meters	.01
square dekameters	square meters	100
	square yards	119.599
square feet	square centimeters	929.0341
	square inches	144
	square meters	.0929
	square yards	.1111
square hectometers	square meters	10,000
square inches	square centimeters	6.4516
	square feet	.00694
	square millimeters	645.1625
	square yards	.00077
square meters	square centimeters	10,000
	square feet	10.7639
	square yards	1.196
square millimeters	square inches	.00155
	square meters	.000001
square yards	square feet	9
	square inches	1296
	square meters	.83613
yards	feet	3
	inches	36
	meters	.9144

MITER ANGLES FOR POLYGONS
(WHEN ALL SIDES ARE EQUAL LENGTH)

For polygons not shown, use the miter angle formula on page 32 to calculate the angle.

Equilateral Triangle
A = 60°
B = 30°

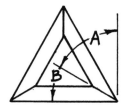

Square (also Rectangle)
A = 45°
B = 45°

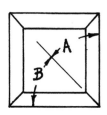

Regular Pentagon
A = 36°
B = 54°

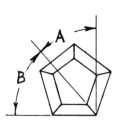

Regular Hexagon
A = 30°
B = 60°

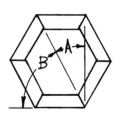

Regular Octagon
A = 22½°
B = 67½°

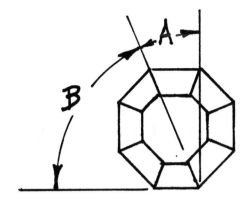

Regular Decagon
A = 18°
B = 72°

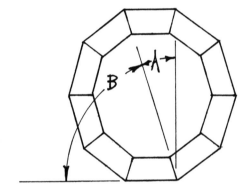

Regular Dodecagon
A = 15°
B = 75°

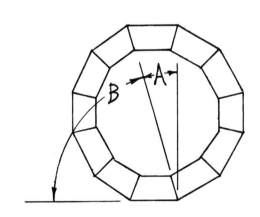

MITER ANGLE FORMULA

For any figure with sides of equal length, use the following formula to calculate the miter angle A:

A = 180/N where:
A = the miter angle (measured from vertical)
N = the number of sides

DETERMINING SIDE LENGTHS FOR POLYGONS

For any figure with sides of equal length, use the following formula to calculate the lengths of the sides:
A = R × C
where:
A = length of side
C = constant (from Constant chart below)
R = radius

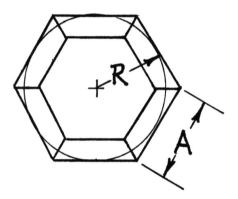

CONSTANT CHART

NUMBER OF EQUAL-LENGTH SIDES	CONSTANT	NUMBER OF EQUAL-LENGTH SIDES	CONSTANT
3 (equilateral triangle)	3.464	8 (regular octagon)	.828
4 (square)	2.000	10 (regular decagon)	.650
5 (regular pentagon)	1.453	12 (regular dodecagon)	.536
6 (regular hexagon)	1.155		

Example: You are making an octagonal wall clock that must be 16″ wide. What length do you cut each of the sides?
   A 16″-wide clock has a radius of 8″.

A = R × C
   = 8 × .828
   = 6.624″ (use 6⅝″)

COMPOUND ANGLES

A compound angle is created by cutting a workpiece at an angle using a saw blade that is also tilted at an angle. The compound angle is commonly used to create tapered-sided boxes and containers. The taper (tilt) angle of the box side is measured from a vertical line. Compound angles can be cut on the table saw or the radial arm saw. Keep in mind, however, that saw gauges are notoriously inaccurate, so it's always best to make test cuts on scrap stock.

The saw blade angle is measured from a vertical line for both the table saw and radial arm saw. The angle of the table saw miter gauge is measured from a line perpendicular to the saw blade. The angle of the radial arm saw is measured from a line perpendicular to the fence.

Not all manufacturers use the same points of reference when establishing the blade tilt and cutting angles shown on their saw gauges. Therefore, the angles marked on your saw gauge might not correspond with the angles shown in the table. To avoid confusion, always set the saw based on angles B and C shown below.

Tilt Angle (A)   **Angle of Blade (B)**

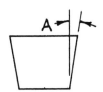
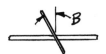

Side View of Box   Table Saw   Radial Arm Saw

Angle of Miter Gauge (C)   **Angle of Radial Arm Saw (C)**

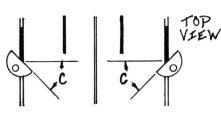
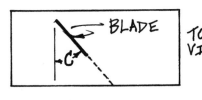

TABLES FOR COMPOUND ANGLES

A = tilt angle of sides
B = blade angle of table or radial-arm saw
C = angle of table saw miter gauge or radial arm saw

FOUR-SIDED FIGURE

A (degrees)	B (degrees)	C (degrees)
5	44.8	4.9
10	44.1	9.9
15	43.1	14.5
20	41.6	18.9
25	39.9	22.9
30	37.8	26.6
35	35.4	29.8
40	32.8	32.7
45	30.0	35.3
50	27.0	37.5
55	23.9	39.3
60	20.7	40.9

FIVE-SIDED FIGURE

A (degrees)	B (degrees)	C (degrees)
5	35.8	3.6
10	35.4	7.2
15	34.6	10.7
20	33.6	14.0
25	32.2	17.1
30	30.6	20.0
35	28.8	22.6
40	26.8	25.0
45	24.6	27.2
50	22.2	29.1
55	19.7	30.8
60	17.1	32.2

SIX-SIDED FIGURE

A (degrees)	B (degrees)	C (degrees)
5	29.9	2.9
10	29.5	5.7
15	28.9	8.5
20	28.0	11.2
25	27.0	13.7
30	25.7	16.1
35	24.2	18.3
40	22.5	20.4
45	20.7	22.2
50	18.8	23.9
55	16.7	25.3
60	14.5	26.6

EIGHT-SIDED FIGURE

A (degrees)	B (degrees)	C (degrees)
5	22.4	2.1
10	22.1	4.1
15	21.7	6.1
20	21.1	8.1
25	20.3	9.9
30	19.4	11.7
35	18.3	13.4
40	17.1	14.9
45	15.7	16.3
50	14.2	17.6
55	12.7	18.7
60	11.0	19.7

A (degrees)	B (degrees)	C (degrees)	A (degrees)	B (degrees)	C (degrees)
5	17.9	1.6	5	14.9.	1.3
10	17.7	3.2	10	14.8	2.7
15	17.4	4.8	15	14.5	4.0
20	16.9	6.3	20	14.1	5.2
25	16.3	7.8	25	13.6	6.5
30	15.5	9.2	30	13.0	7.6
35	14.7	10.6	35	12.2	8.7
40	13.7	11.8	40	11.4	9.8
45	12.6	12.9	45	10.6	10.7
50	11.5	14.0	50	9.6	11.6
55	10.2	14.9	55	8.5	12.4
60	8.9	15.7	60	7.4	13.1

ENLARGING GRID PATTERNS USING A PHOTOCOPY MACHINE
(ACCURATE TO WITHIN 1 PERCENT. PHOTOCOPY MACHINE MUST BE ABLE TO ENLARGE AT LEAST 150 PERCENT.)

A photocopy machine can be a real timesaver when enlarging a grid pattern. The table shown here requires the use of a photocopy machine that can enlarge at least 150 percent. If you don't have easy access to such a machine, your local copy center is likely to have one.

You'll need to determine the percentage of enlargement before you can use the table. To determine the percentage of enlargement:

1. Determine the desired full-size length of the pattern.
2. Measure the length of the pattern on the grid.
3. Divide the desired full-size length by the measured length of pattern on the grid, then multiply by 100.

Example: Plans for a hutch cupboard show a grid pattern for a curved bracket foot. The full-size curve must measure 6″ long. On the pattern, the curve measures 1⅞″ long. How much must the curve be enlarged to produce a full-size pattern?

Percentage of enlargement = desired full-size length/measured length of pattern
on grid × 100
= 6/1⅞ × 100
= 3.2 × 100
= 320 percent

Once the percentage of enlargement is known, the table on the next two pages details how to enlarge the pattern using a photocopier.

TO ENLARGE ORIGINAL BY: (percentage of enlargement)	STEP 1 Photocopy original at this percentage:	STEP 2 Photocopy 1st copy at this percentage:	STEP 3 Photocopy 2nd copy at this percentage:	STEP 4 Photocopy 3rd copy at this percentage:
155	150	103	–	–
160	150	107	–	–
165	150	110	–	–
170	150	113	–	–
175	150	117	–	–
180	150	120	–	–
185	150	123	–	–
190	150	127	–	–
195	150	130	–	–
200	150	133	–	–
205	150	137	–	–
210	150	140	–	–
215	150	143	–	–
220	150	147	–	–
225	150	150	–	–
230	150	150	102	–
235	150	150	104	–
240	150	150	107	–
245	150	150	109	–
250	150	150	111	–
255	150	150	113	–
260	150	150	116	–
265	150	150	118	–
270	150	150	120	–
275	150	150	122	–
280	150	150	124	–
285	150	150	127	–
290	150	150	129	–
295	150	150	131	–
300	150	150	133	–
305	150	150	136	–
310	150	150	138	–
315	150	150	140	–
320	150	150	142	–
325	150	150	144	–
330	150	150	147	–
335	150	150	149	–
340	150	150	150	101
345	150	150	150	102

TO ENLARGE ORIGINAL BY: (percentage of enlargement)	STEP 1 Photocopy original at this percentage:	STEP 2 Photocopy 1st copy at this percentage:	STEP 3 Photocopy 2nd copy at this percentage:	STEP 4 Photocopy 3rd copy at this percentage:
350	150	150	150	104
355	150	150	150	105
360	150	150	150	107
365	150	150	150	108
370	150	150	148	111
375	150	150	150	111
380	150	150	148	114
385	150	150	150	114
390	150	150	148	117
395	150	150	150	117
400	150	150	148	120

CIRCLE TEMPLATES AROUND THE HOUSE

Looking for a circle template? As shown here, the template you need might be in your kitchen cupboard, workshop cabinet or even your pants pocket.

TEMPLATE	DIAMETER (inches)	RADIUS (inches)
penny	$3/4$	$3/8$
nickel	$7/8$	$7/16$
quarter	1	$1/2$
top end of 35mm film canister	$1 3/8$	$11/16$
lid from 1 gallon plastic milk container	$1 1/2$	$3/4$
bottom end of Old Spice shave cream (11 oz. can)	$1 5/8$	$13/16$
bottom end of WD-40 (9 oz. can)	$2 3/4$	$1 3/8$
bottom end of Minwax Wood Finish ($1/2$ pint can)	$2 7/8$	$1 7/16$
bottom end of Borden's condensed milk (12 oz. can)	3	$1 1/2$
bottom end of Minwax Wood Finish (1 pint can)	$3 3/8$	$1 11/16$
bottom end of Folger's coffee (12 oz. can)	4	2
bottom end of Butcher's Wax (16 oz. can)	$4 1/4$	$2 1/8$
bottom end of Cabot's Wood Stain (1 gal. can)	$6 3/4$	$3 3/8$

CHAPTER 2

FURNITURE DESIGN

COMMON WOODWORKING JOINTS

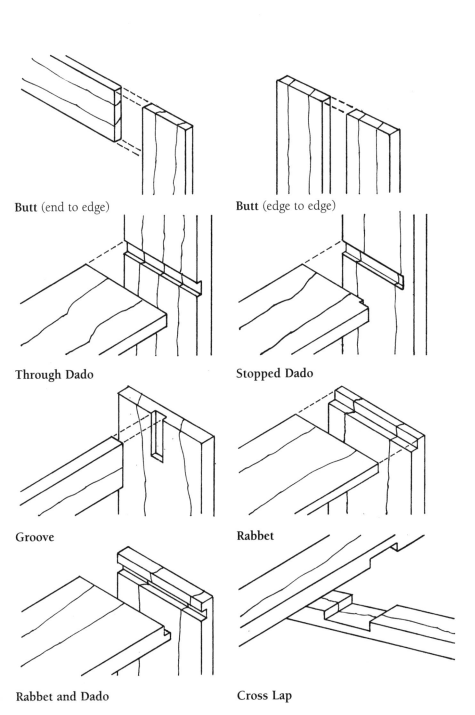

Butt (end to edge)

Butt (edge to edge)

Through Dado

Stopped Dado

Groove

Rabbet

Rabbet and Dado

Cross Lap

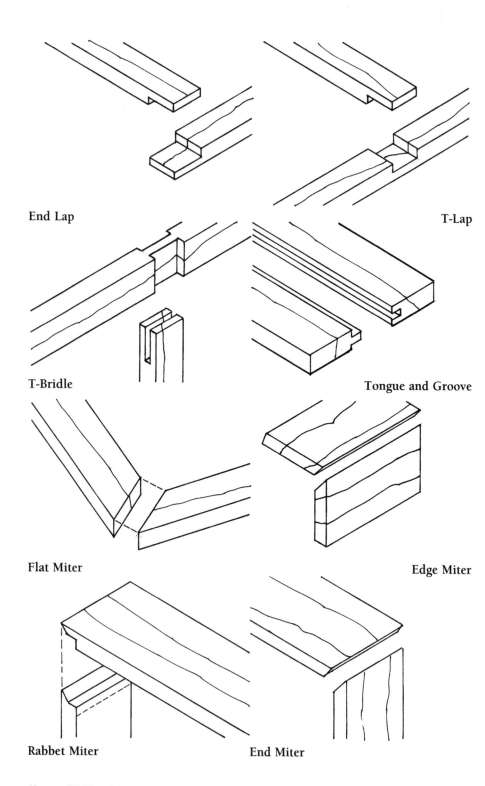

End Lap

T-Lap

T-Bridle

Tongue and Groove

Flat Miter

Edge Miter

Rabbet Miter

End Miter

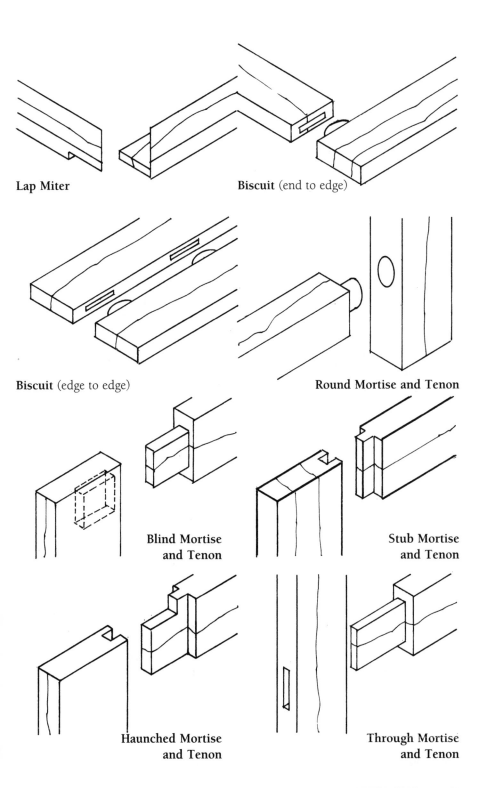

Lap Miter

Biscuit (end to edge)

Biscuit (edge to edge)

Round Mortise and Tenon

Blind Mortise and Tenon

Stub Mortise and Tenon

Haunched Mortise and Tenon

Through Mortise and Tenon

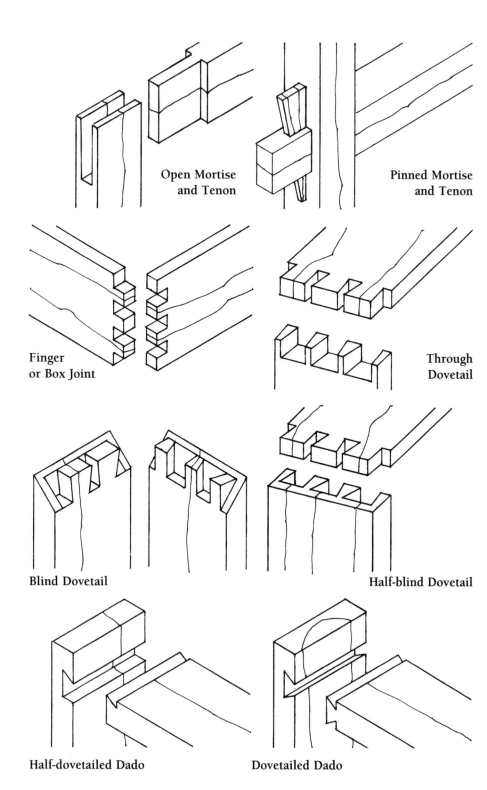

Open Mortise and Tenon

Pinned Mortise and Tenon

Finger or Box Joint

Through Dovetail

Blind Dovetail

Half-blind Dovetail

Half-dovetailed Dado

Dovetailed Dado

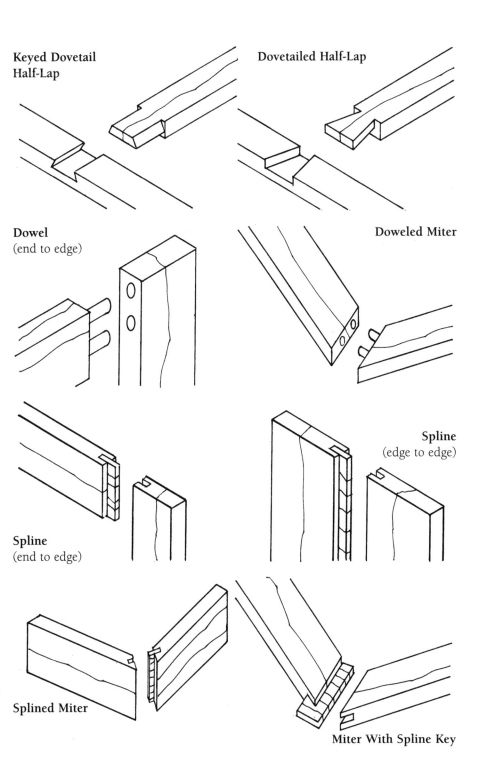

Keyed Dovetail Half-Lap

Dovetailed Half-Lap

Dowel
(end to edge)

Doweled Miter

Spline
(edge to edge)

Spline
(end to edge)

Splined Miter

Miter With Spline Key

GENERAL RULES FOR JOINERY DESIGN

A number of general rules, or rules of thumb, can be applied to the design of wood-working joints. Although they work just fine for most applications, keep in mind that these rules are not absolute, so there will be occasional exceptions.

MORTISE AND TENON JOINTS

- When the mating parts are the same thickness, make the tenon about one-third the stock thickness.
- When cutting a blind mortise and tenon, make the mortise $1/16''$ to $1/8''$ deeper than the tenon length. The added space provides room for any excess glue to collect, allowing the joint to fully close when clamp pressure is applied.

DOVETAILS

- The dovetail angle affects both strength and appearance. Avoid a dovetail angle of less than 7° because the resulting joint offers minimal locking strength. Also, avoid a dovetail angle that's more than 14° as the resulting short-grain edges are more likely to shear off if the joint is heavily stressed. Any angle between 9° and 11° offers good strength and appearance. A 7° angle produces an attractive dovetail, but it should only be used when a joint is subjected to little stress. Since dovetail angles are often specified as slopes, the chart below lists common dovetail angles and their approximate slopes.

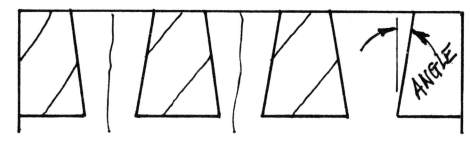

DOVETAIL ANGLE (degrees)	APPROXIMATE SLOPE
7	1:8
8	1:7
9	1:6
11	1:5
14	1:4

DOWEL JOINTS

- Use a dowel diameter that's between one-third and one-half the stock thickness (for example use a ¼, ⁵⁄₁₆ or ⅜″ diameter dowel for ¾″ thick stock).
- When boring dowel holes, add ¹⁄₁₆″ clearance at each end to allow for excess glue.
- When using dowels to help align edge-to-edge joints, space the dowels 8″ to 12″ apart.

LAP JOINTS

- When the mating parts are the same thickness, the lap should be one-half the stock thickness.

NAIL JOINTS

- When nailing a thinner piece to a thicker piece, the nail length should be about three times the thickness of the thinner piece. Example: Use a 2¼″ long nail to attach a piece of ¾″ thick stock to a piece of 3½″ thick stock.
- When both parts are about the same thickness, the nail length should be ⅛″ to ¼″ less than the combined thicknesses of the parts. Example: Use a 2¾″ long nail to join two pieces of 1½″ thick stock.
- When nailing near the end of a board, drill pilot holes to prevent the stock from splitting. The pilot hole diameter should be about 75 percent of the nail diameter and bored to a depth of about two-thirds the nail length.

SCREW JOINTS

- About two-thirds of the screw (or the entire thread length) should enter the mating piece.
- When both parts are about the same thickness, the screw length should be ⅛″ to ¼″ less than the combined thicknesses of the parts. Example: Use a 1⅝″ long screw when joining a ¾″ thick piece to a 1″ thick piece.

STANDARD FURNITURE DIMENSIONS

Most chairs, dining tables and desktops are designed to be used by average-size adults. Other furniture size standards are dictated by the intended use. Coffee tables are relatively low in order to be at a convenient height when used in front of a sofa. Sofa table heights are dictated by the heights of sofa backs. Night tables are designed to put a lamp at a comfortable elevation for reading in bed.

The illustrations that follow show the standard sizes for a variety of furniture pieces. Keep in mind, though, that sometimes there can be good reasons to make exceptions. If you are shorter or taller than average, you can ignore the standard chair heights and build a chair that's perfect for your size.

CHAIRS

Chairs can vary considerably in size, shape, style and utility. Chair seats can be square or rectangular, but just as often they are wider in the front than in the back. Chair backs are usually angled several degrees to improve comfort, although occasionally the back is at a right angle to the seat. Then, too, there are endless varieties of back and leg configurations. However, despite the fact that there are many ways to build a chair, the basic dimensions should conform to the figures shown here.

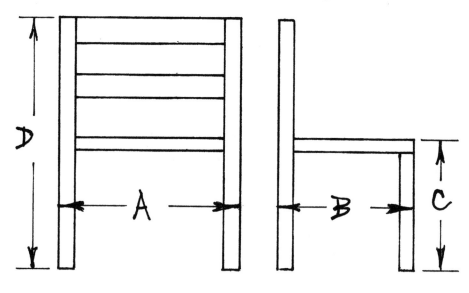

DIMENSIONS (in inches)	A	B	C	D
kitchen	14–16	14–16	17–18½	30–36
dining—side	18–21	16–20	18–18½	40–48
dining—arm	20–27	16–20	18–18½	40–48

DINING TABLES

The standard dimensions shown here apply to square, rectangular and round dining tables. Note that the table size is influenced by the number of seated persons and the amount of space allotted for each person. All dimensions are in inches.

Square Tables

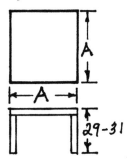

PEOPLE	MINIMUM SPACE (A)	AVERAGE SPACE (A)	AMPLE SPACE (A)
2	24	28	32
4	34	38	42
8	44	48	52

Rectangular Tables

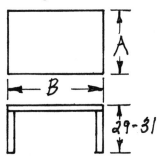

PEOPLE	MINIMUM SPACE		AVERAGE SPACE		AMPLE SPACE	
	(A)	(B)	(A)	(B)	(A)	(B)
2	22	28	24	30	28	32
4	28	44	32	48	36	52
6	34	50	36	66	42	72
8	34	72	36	86	42	90

Round Tables

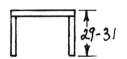

PEOPLE	MINIMUM SPACE (A)	AVERAGE SPACE (A)	AMPLE SPACE (A)
2	22	24	28
4	32	36	42
6	42	50	54
8	56	62	72

OTHER TABLES

Many tables are designed to have a specific use in the home. Dimensions for some of the more common ones are shown here.

Occasional Table   End Table

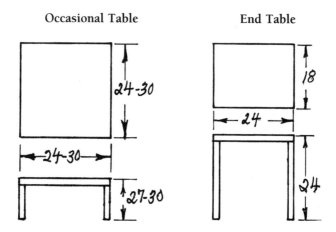

Coffee Table

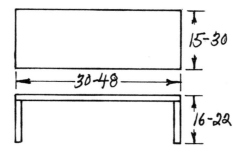

Sofa (Hunt) Table

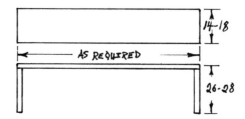

DESKS

The dimensions of desktops can vary widely, so the length and width figures shown should only serve as a general guide. However, the desk height dimension is based on what is considered to be a comfortable working height for most people, so it should be adhered to pretty closely.

Writing Desks

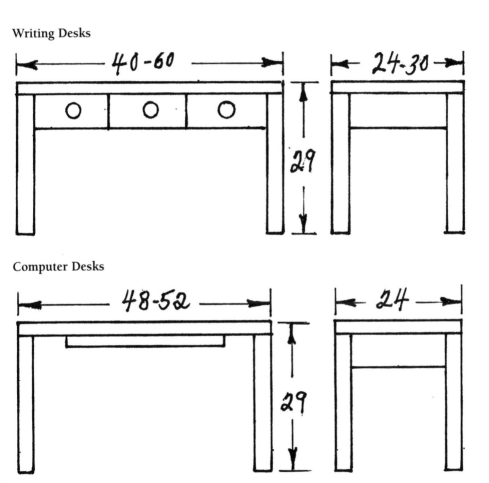

Computer Desks

BEDS

The length and width dimensions represent the distances measured to the inside of the frame. The figures are based on the standard dimensions for twin, double, queen- and king-size beds.

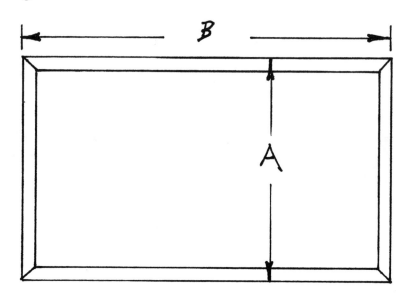

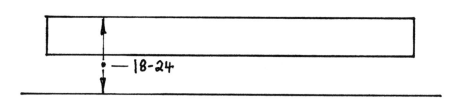

SIZE	DIMENSIONS	
	A (inches)	B (inches)
Twin (Single)	39	75
Double (Full)	54	75
Queen	60	80
King	76	80

SHELVES

When determining shelf heights, keep in mind that you should be able to reach items on a shelf without having to use a stepstool or stand on your toes. The range of heights shown here takes into account the fact that all people are not the same height. If the shelves are to be regularly used by someone under 5'6" tall, use the lower figures.

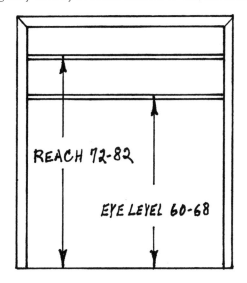

WORKBENCHES

Workbench widths and lengths are not standardized. That's because the best bench-top size is likely to be determined by individual needs and the available space in the workshop. Commercial bench manufacturers understand this. Indeed, you'll find that commercial benches range from a compact 16"×36" to a substantial 24"×90", with a range of sizes in between. My bench, which I find to be a useful size for my shop, measures 30"×60".

While benchtop sizes are widely variable, workbench heights are another matter. A workbench should be at a height that you'll find comfortable for planing, sawing, sanding and other woodworking operations. Commercial benches range in height from 33" to 35". However, if you plan to make a bench for your own use, you'll have the luxury of building it to a height that's best suited for your size.

You can pretty closely determine the workbench height that's best suited for your size by standing straight with your arms hanging down at your sides. Turn the palms of your hands so they are parallel to the floor, then measure the distance from the floor to your palms. For most woodworkers, this method results in a comfortable bench height for most operations.

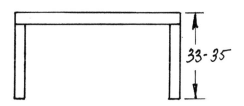

KITCHEN CABINETS

Kitchen cabinet dimensions have been standardized to ensure maximum convenience. Most kitchen appliances are designed for use with these standard sizes.

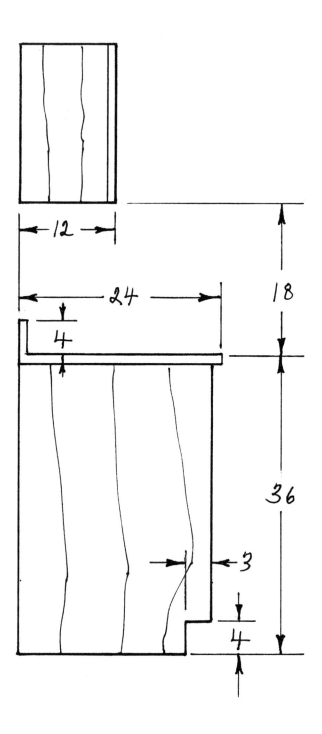

UNDERSTANDING A SHOP DRAWING

Small Footstool—Illustration

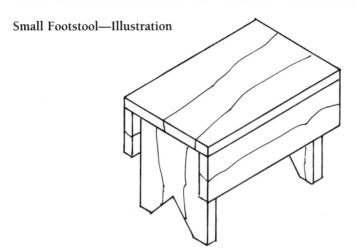

Orthographic View

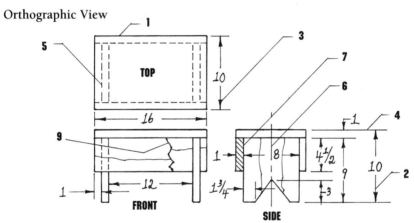

1. Outline—A heavy line representing the important visible surfaces of a part.
2. Dimension Line—A thin line, broken at the center and terminating with arrows at each end. Used to indicate length.
3. Arrowhead—Symbol used to indicate the ends of a dimension line.
4. Extension Line—Thin lines extending from (but not touching) a part and used to establish the ends of a dimension line.
5. Dotted Line—A heavy broken line representing the important surfaces of a part that are hidden from view. Also called a hidden line.
6. Centerline—Light line used to indicate the center of surfaces, circles and arcs.
7. Sectional Lines—Light parallel lines drawn to indicate surfaces that have been sectioned.
8. Long Break Line (not shown)—Zigzag line used to indicate that a part has been shortened, allowing the part to fit better on a shop drawing.
9. Short Break Line—Zigzag line used to shorten a part, usually to expose a hidden component.

A typical shop drawing shows the footstool as viewed from the front, side and top. Such multi-view drawings are generally called orthographic views. A relatively simple project might only require a front and side view in order to provide the necessary information. However, a more complicated project often requires views from the front, back, top and both sides.

A sectional view, sometimes called a section, is often used to show the profile of a hidden part. To understand a sectional view, you need to imagine that the part has been cut in two along an imaginary cutting plane. Then, too, imagine that you remove the front of the part that was cut. The part that remains represents what is shown in a sectional view. Shop drawings sometimes include an exploded view (not shown). Exploded views can be helpful, especially when used with complicated projects, because they provide a three-dimensional perspective.

COMMON WOODWORKING ABBREVIATIONS

ABBREVIATION	MEANING	ABBREVIATION	MEANING
AD	air dried	cyl.	cylinder
amp.	amperes	D	diameter
aux.	auxiliary	db.	decibel
avdp.	avoirdupois	deg.	degree
bd. ft.	board foot	dia.	diameter
bev.	bevel	diam.	diameter
B/M	bill of materials	dr.	dram
brs.	brass	dwl.	dowel
C	centigrade	F	Fahrenheit
cg	centigram	FAS	firsts and seconds
cl	centiliter	F.H.	flathead
cbore	counterbore	F.H.W.S.	flathead wood screw
c'bore	counterbore	fl.	fluid
cham.	chamfer	ft.	foot
cir.	circle	fpm	feet per minute
CL	centerline	fps	feet per second
cm	centimeter	g	gram
csk	countersink	gal.	gallon
c'sink	countersink	galv.	galvanized
cu.	cubic	gpm	gallons per minute

ABBREVIATION	MEANING	ABBREVIATION	MEANING
hex	hexagon	R	radius
hp	horsepower	R.H.	roundhead
hr.	hour	R.H.W.S.	roundhead wood screw
I.D.	inside diameter		
in.	inch	rd.	round
KD	kiln-dried	rpm	revolutions per minute
kg	kilogram		
kl	kiloliter	rps	revolutions per second
km	kilometer		
l	liter	S1E	surfaced one edge
lb.	pound	S2E	surfaced two edges
m	meter	S1S	surfaced one side
MC (or M.C.)	moisture content	S2S	surfaced two sides
mg	milligram	S4S	surfaced four sides
mldg.	molding	S1S1E	surfaced one side, one edge
mm	millimeter		
min.	minute	S1S2E	surfaced one side, two edges
misc.	miscellaneous		
OAL	overall length	S2S1E	surfaced two sides, one edge
O.H.	oval head		
O.H.W.S.	oval head wood screw	sec.	second
O.D.	outside diameter	SEL	select grade
oz.	ounce	scr.	screw
ply.	plywood	sq.	square
ppm	parts per million	stl.	steel
pt.	pint	std.	standard
psf	pounds per square foot	temp.	temperature
		T&G	tongue and groove
psi	pounds per square inch	thd.	thread
		tpi	teeth per inch
qt.	quart	V	volt
rad.	radius	yd.	yard

COMMON WOODWORKING SYMBOLS

SYMBOL	MEANING	SYMBOL	MEANING
+	add (plus)	₡	centerline
−	subtract (minus)	⌐	right angle
×	multiply		
÷	divide		
=	equals		
#	pounds (also number)		
%	percent		
°	degrees		
′	foot		
″	inch		

PARTICLEBOARD SHELF SPANS

Particleboard is commonly used as a shelving material. Typically, shelves are exposed to two types of loads—uniform and concentrated. A uniform load is one that is applied across the entire length of a shelf. A shelf filled with books is an example of uniform loading. On the other hand, a concentrated load is one that is applied to a relatively small area. Placing a belt sander in the middle of an empty shelf is an example of a concentrated load.

Use the formulas and chart on pages 57–58 to determine the maximum uniform and concentrated loads for various lengths and thicknesses of grade M-2 particleboard. The chart offers five thickness options: ½, ⅝, ¾, 1 and 1⅛″. The chart also shows the maximum deflection (sag) when the given shelf length is at maximum uniform load.

The chart is based on having end supports that are securely anchored. Supports are most effective when they extend across the full width of the shelf.

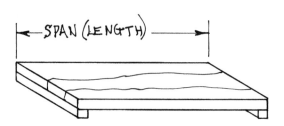

UNIFORM LOADS

For uniform loads, use the following formula:

Uniform load = expected load on the shelf (in pounds)/area of shelf (in square feet)

Example: What is the uniform load on a 6″ wide by 36″ long grade M-2 particleboard shelf that is expected to support 60 pounds of books?

1. Calculate the area of the shelf.

Area of shelf = shelf width × shelf length
= 6″×36″
= 216 square inches

Convert square inches to square feet (see conversion table on page 29).

Area of shelf = 216 square inches × .00694 = 1.5 square feet

2. Calculate the uniform load.

Uniform load = 60 pounds/1.5 square feet
= 40 pounds per square foot (psf)

Once the uniform load is known, use the chart on page 58 to determine the thickness and maximum shelf length that can be used. As shown, for a uniform load of 40 psf, you have several shelf options: ½″ thick by no more than 16″ long, ⅝″ thick by no more than 20″ long, ¾″ thick by no more than 24″ long, 1″ thick by no more than 32″ long and 1⅛″ thick by no more than 36″ long.

CONCENTRATED LOADS

For a concentrated load, add a safety factor by dividing the expected load on the shelf by .625, then use the uniform load formula.

Example: You want to place a 60-pound workshop dehumidifier by itself in the center of a ¾″ thick by 10″ wide by 36″ long grade M-2 particleboard shelf. Can the shelf support the concentrated load?

1. Calculate the concentrated load safety factor.

Concentrated load safety factor = expected load on shelf (in pounds)/.625
= 60 pounds/.625
= 96 pounds

2. Calculate the shelf area.

Area of shelf = shelf width × shelf length
= 10″×36″
= 360 square inches

Convert square inches to square feet (see conversion table on page 29).

Area of shelf = 360 square inches × .00694 = 2.5 square feet

3. Calculate the uniform load.

Uniform load = expected load on the shelf (in pounds)/area of shelf (in square feet)

= 96 pounds/2.5 square feet

= 38.4 psf

As shown in the chart, a ¾″ thick by 36″ long shelf can only support a uniform load of 10 pounds. However, 1⅛″ thick particleboard can support 45 pounds per square foot. Replace the ¾″ particleboard with 1⅛″ thick particleboard.

MAXIMUM LOADS FOR PARTICLEBOARD SHELVING

For uniformly loaded grade M-2 particleboard.

SHELF SPAN (inches)	MAXIMUM DEFLECTION (inches)	UNIFORM LOAD (pounds per square foot) FOR SHELF THICKNESS (inches):				
		½	⅝	¾	1	1⅛
16	.089	45	95	124	166	186
20	.111	20	45	80	130	146
24	.133	13	25	45	107	120
28	.156	8	15	25	70	100
32	.178	—	10	18	45	65
36	.200	—	5	10	30	45
40	.222	—	—	8	20	30
44	.244	—	—	5	15	25
48	.267	—	—	—	10	15
52	.289	—	—	—	8	10
56	.311	—	—	—	5	8
60	.333	—	—	—	—	5

Chart courtesy of the National Particleboard Association.

FACTORY-MADE PINE MOLDINGS

The moldings shown here don't represent all the standard pine moldings that are available, but they are the ones most likely to have furniture applications. If not in stock, most retailers can special-order them for you. The most common sizes are shown. Other sizes might be available—check your retailer.

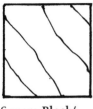

Square Block/
Baluster

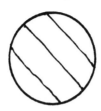

Full Round

Band

Base

Base Cap

Floor/Shoe

Bed

Neck

COMMONLY AVAILABLE SIZES

Square Block/Baluster
3/4" × 3/4"
1 1/8" × 1 1/8"
1 3/8" × 1 3/8"
1 5/8" × 1 5/8"

Full Round
1 1/8"
1 3/8" (closet pole)
1 5/8"

Band
11/16" × 1 5/8"

Base
11/16" × 11/16"

Base Cap
11/16" × 1 1/8"
11/16" × 1 3/8"

Floor/Shoe
1/2" × 3/4"

Bed
9/16" × 1 5/8"
9/16" × 2 1/4"
9/16" × 2 5/8"

Neck
5/8" × 3/4"

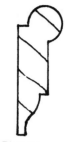

Nose and Cove   Chair Rail   Picture

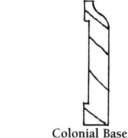

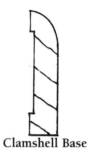

Colonial Base   Clamshell Base

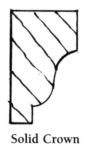

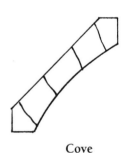

Crown   Solid Crown   Cove

COMMONLY AVAILABLE SIZES

Nose and Cove
$3/8'' \times 1/2''$
$1/2'' \times 5/8''$
$5/8'' \times 3/4''$

Chair Rail
$11/16'' \times 21/2''$

Picture
$11/16'' \times 1 3/8''$

Colonial Base
$9/16'' \times 3 1/4''$

Clamshell Base
$9/16'' \times 3 1/4''$

Crown
$9/16'' \times 2 5/8''$
$9/16'' \times 3 5/8''$
$11/16'' \times 4 1/2''$

Solid Crown
$11/16'' \times 1 5/8''$
$1 1/8'' \times 2 1/4''$

Cove
$9/16'' \times 1 5/8''$
$11/16'' \times 2 5/8''$

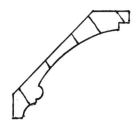

Beaded Cove

Colonial Stop

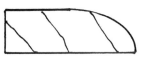

Clamshell Stop

Sanitary Stop

Bullnose Stop

Quarter Round

Half Round

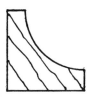

Cove Mold

COMMONLY AVAILABLE SIZES

Beaded Cove	Clamshell Stop	Quarter Round	Half Round
$^{11}/_{16}'' \times 1^5/_8''$	$^3/_8'' \times ^3/_4''$	$^1/_4''$	$^1/_2''$
$^{11}/_{16}'' \times 2^5/_8''$	$^3/_8'' \times ^7/_8''$	$^3/_8''$	$^5/_8''$
	$^3/_8'' \times 1\,^3/_8''$	$^1/_2''$	$^3/_4''$
Colonial Stop	$^3/_8'' \times 1^5/_8''$	$^5/_8''$	$1^1/_8''$
$^3/_8'' \times ^3/_4''$		$^3/_4''$	$1^3/_8''$
$^3/_8'' \times ^7/_8''$	**Sanitary Stop**	$^7/_8''$	
$^3/_8'' \times 1^1/_8''$	$^3/_8'' \times 1^3/_8''$	$1^1/_8''$	**Cove Mold**
$^3/_8'' \times 1^3/_8''$			$^1/_2'' \times ^1/_2''$
$^3/_8'' \times 1^5/_8''$	**Bullnose Stop**		$^5/_8'' \times ^3/_4''$
$^3/_8'' \times 2^1/_4''$	$^3/_8'' \times 1^5/_8''$		$^{11}/_{16}'' \times ^{11}/_{16}''$
			$^{11}/_{16}'' \times ^7/_8''$
			$^{11}/_{16}'' \times 1^1/_8''$

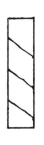

Lattice

Screen (Flat)

Screen (3-Bead)

Screen (2-Bead)

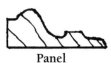

Panel

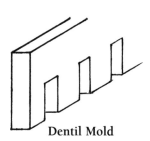

Dentil Mold

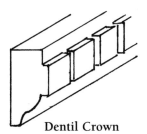

Dentil Crown

COMMONLY AVAILABLE SIZES

Lattice
$1/4'' \times 1 1/8''$
$1/4'' \times 1 3/8''$
$1/4'' \times 1 5/8''$
$1/4'' \times 2''$
$1/4'' \times 2 5/8''$

Screen (Flat)
$1/4'' \times 3/4''$

Screen (3-Bead)
$1/4'' \times 3/4''$

Screen (2-Bead)
$1/4'' \times 5/8''$

Panel
$3/8'' \times 1''$

Dentil Mold
$1/2'' \times 2''$

Dentil Crown
$3/4'' \times 1 5/8''$

WOOD SCREW SHANK AND PILOT HOLE DRILL SIZES

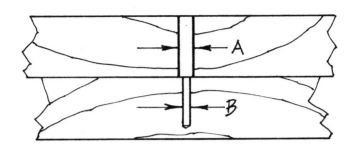

SCREW NUMBER	SHANK HOLE DRILL SIZE (A) (inches)	SOFTWOOD PILOT HOLE DRILL SIZE (B) (inches)	HARDWOOD PILOT HOLE DRILL SIZE (B) (inches)
0	1/16	—	1/32
1	5/64	1/32	1/32
2	3/32	1/32	3/64
3	7/64	3/64	1/16
4	7/64	3/64	1/16
5	1/8	1/16	5/64
6	9/64	1/16	5/64
7	5/32	5/64	3/32
8	11/64	5/64	3/32
9	3/16	3/32	7/64
10	3/16	3/32	7/64
12	7/32	7/64	1/8
14	1/4	7/64	9/64
16	17/64	1/8	5/32
18	19/64	9/64	3/16
20	21/64	5/32	13/64
24	3/8	3/16	7/32

LAG SCREW SHANK AND PILOT HOLE DRILL SIZES

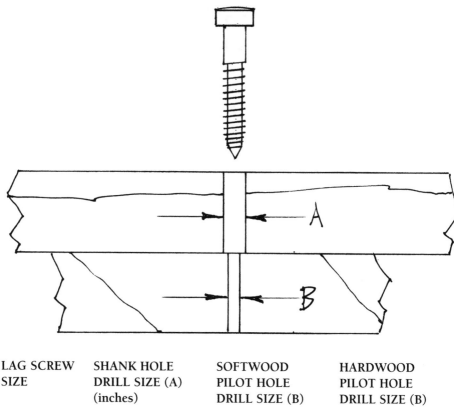

LAG SCREW SIZE	SHANK HOLE DRILL SIZE (A) (inches)	SOFTWOOD PILOT HOLE DRILL SIZE (B) (inches)	HARDWOOD PILOT HOLE DRILL SIZE (B) (inches)
$3/16$	$3/16$	$7/64$	$1/8$
$1/4$	$1/4$	$5/32$	$11/64$
$5/16$	$5/16$	$3/16$	$7/32$
$3/8$	$3/8$	$7/32$	$17/64$
$7/16$	$7/16$	$17/64$	$5/16$
$1/2$	$1/2$	$19/64$	$11/32$

THREADED INSERT (ROSAN NUT) PILOT HOLE DRILL SIZES
(FOR HARDWOOD AND SOFTWOOD)

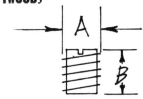

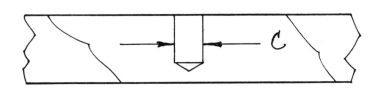

INTERNAL THREAD	MAJOR DIAMETER OF EXTERNAL THREAD (A) (inches)	LENGTH (B) (inches)	PILOT HOLE DRILL SIZE (C) (inches)
4-40	.350	$3/8$	$1/4$
6-32	.350	$3/8$	$1/4$
8-32	.350	$3/8$	$1/4$
10-24	.453	$1/2$	$3/8$
10-32	.453	$1/2$	$3/8$
$1/4$-20	.453	$1/2$	$3/8$
$5/16$-18	.594	$9/16$	$1/2$
$3/8$-16	.600	$5/8$	$1/2$

CLEAR GLASS
COMMONLY AVAILABLE THICKNESSES

Inches	Millimeters
$3/32$	2.5
$1/8$	3.0
$5/32$	4.0
$3/16$	5.0
$1/4$	6.0
$5/16$	8.0
$3/8$	10.0
$1/2$	12.0

ACRYLIC SHEET

This product is sold under several trade names, including Plexiglas.

COMMONLY AVAILABLE THICKNESSES

Inches	Millimeters
.080	2.0
.100	2.5
1/8	3.0
3/16	5.0
1/4	6.0

PLASTIC LAMINATE

Plastic laminate is sold under several trade names, including Formica. Some of the commonly used grades are shown below. A variety of finishes are available. See your local dealer for information on other grades.

GRADE	THICKNESS (inches)	TYPICAL USE
10	.050	Horizontal and vertical interior applications. Most widely used grade.
12	.042	Horizontal interior applications that require forming. Minimum outside radius: 1/2". Minimum inside radius: 3/8".
20	.030	Vertical or light-duty horizontal interior applications that require forming. Minimum outside and inside radius: 3/8".
30	.039	Vertical or light-duty horizontal interior applications. Can be formed. Minimum outside and inside radius: 1/2".
32	.032	Vertical and horizontal interior applications that require low flame spread ratings.

CHAPTER 3

WOOD

COMMERCIAL, COMMON, AND BOTANICAL NAMES FOR DOMESTIC COMMERCIAL HARDWOODS

COMMERCIAL NAME	COMMON TREE NAME	BOTANICAL NAME
Alder, Red	Red Alder	Alnus rubra
Ash, Black	Black Ash	Fraxinus nigra
Ash, Oregon	Oregon Ash	Fraxinus latifolia
Ash, White	Blue Ash	Fraxinus quadrangulata
Ash, White	Green Ash	Fraxinus pennsylvanica
Ash, White	White Ash	Fraxinus americana
Aspen (Popple)	Bigtooth Aspen	Populus grandidentata
Aspen (Popple)	Quaking Aspen	Populus tremuloides
Basswood	American Basswood	Tilia americana
Basswood	White Basswood	Tilia heterophylla
Beech	American Beech	Fagus grandifolia
Birch	Gray Birch	Betula populifolia
Birch	Paper Birch	Betula papyrifera
Birch	River Birch	Betula nigra
Birch	Sweet Birch	Betula lenta
Birch	Yellow Birch	Betula alleghaniensis
Box Elder	Box Elder	Acer negundo
Buckeye	Ohio Buckeye	Aesculus glabra
Buckeye	Yellow Buckeye	Aesculus octandra
Butternut	Butternut	Juglans cinerea
Cherry	Black Cherry	Prunus serotina
Chestnut	American Chestnut	Castanea dentata
Cottonwood	Balsam Poplar	Populus balsamifera
Cottonwood	Eastern Cottonwood	Populus deltoides
Cottonwood	Black Cottonwood	Populus trichocarpa
Cucumber	Cucumber Tree	Magnolia acuminata
Dogwood	Flowering Dogwood	Cornus florida
Dogwood	Pacific Dogwood	Cornus nuttallii
Elm, Rock	Cedar Elm	Ulmus crassifolia
Elm, Rock	Rock Elm	Ulmus thomasii
Elm, Rock	September Elm	Ulmus serotina
Elm, Rock	Winged Elm	Ulmus alata

COMMERCIAL NAME	COMMON TREE NAME	BOTANICAL NAME
Elm, Soft	American Elm	Ulmus americana
Elm, Soft	Slippery Elm	Ulmus rubra
Gum	Sweet Gum	Liquidambar styraciflua
Hackberry	Hackberry	Celtis occidentalis
Hackberry	Sugarberry	Celtis laevigata
Hickory	Mockernut Hickory	Carya tomentosa
Hickory	Pignut Hickory	Carya glabra
Hickory	Shagbark Hickory	Carya ovata
Hickory	Shellbark Hickory	Carya laciniosa
Holly	American Holly	Ilex opaca
Ironwood	Eastern Hop Hornbeam	Ostrya virginiana
Locust	Black Locust	Robinia pseudoacacia
Locust	Honey Locust	Gleditsia triacanthos
Madrone	Pacific Madrone	Arbutus menziesii
Magnolia	Southern Magnolia	Magnolia grandiflora
Magnolia	Sweet Bay	Magnolia virginiana
Maple, Hard	Black Maple	Acer nigrum
Maple, Hard	Sugar Maple	Acer saccharum
Maple, Oregon	Big Leaf Maple	Acer macrophyllum
Maple, Soft	Red Maple	Acer rubrum
Maple, Soft	Silver Maple	Acer saccharinum
Oak, Red	Black Oak	Quercus velutina
Oak, Red	Blackjack Oak	Quercus marilandica
Oak, Red	California Black Oak	Quercus kelloggi
Oak, Red	Laurel Oak	Quercus laurifolia
Oak, Red	Northern Pin Oak	Quercus ellipsoidalis
Oak, Red	Northern Red Oak	Quercus rubra
Oak, Red	Nuttail Oak	Quercus nuttallii
Oak, Red	Pin Oak	Quercus palustris
Oak, Red	Scarlet Oak	Quercus coccinea
Oak, Red	Shumard Oak	Quercus shumardii
Oak, Red	Southern Red Oak	Quercus falcata
Oak, Red	Turkey Oak	Quercus laevis
Oak, Red	Willow Oak	Quercus phellos
Oak, White	Arizona White Oak	Quercus arizonica
Oak, White	Blue Oak	Quercus douglasii
Oak, White	Burr Oak	Quercus macrocarpa
Oak, White	Valley Oak	Quercus lobata
Oak, White	Chestnut Oak	Quercus prinus

COMMERCIAL NAME	COMMON TREE NAME	BOTANICAL NAME
Oak, White	Chinkapin Oak	Quercus muehlenbergii
Oak, White	Emory Oak	Quercus emoryi
Oak, White	Gambel Oak	Quercus gambelii
Oak, White	Mexican Blue Oak	Quercus oblongifolia
Oak, White	Live Oak	Quercus virginiana
Oak, White	Oregon White Oak	Quercus garryana
Oak, White	Overcup Oak	Quercus lyrata
Oak, White	Post Oak	Quercus stellata
Oak, White	Swamp Chestnut Oak	Quercus michauxii
Oak, White	Swamp White Oak	Quercus bicolor
Oak, White	White Oak	Quercus alba
Oregon Myrtle	California Laurel	Umbellularia californica
Osage Orange	Osage Orange	Maclura pomifera
Pecan	Bitternut Hickory	Carya cordiformis
Pecan	Nutmeg Hickory	Carya myristicaeformis
Pecan	Water Hickory	Carya aquatica
Pecan	Pecan	Carya illinoensis
Persimmon	Common Persimmon	Diospyros virginiana
Poplar	Yellow Poplar	Liriodendron tulipifera
Sassafras	Sassafras	Sassafras albidum
Sycamore	American Sycamore	Platanus occidentalis
Tan Oak	Tan Oak	Lithocarpus densiflorus
Tupelo	Black Tupelo, Blackgum	Nyssa sylvatica
Tupelo	Ogeechee Tupelo	Nyssa ogeche
Tupelo	Water Tupelo	Nyssa aquatica
Walnut	Black Walnut	Juglans nigra
Willow	Black Willow	Salix nigra
Willow	Peach Leaf Willow	Salix amygdaloides

STANDARD, FOREST SERVICE, AND BOTANICAL NAMES FOR DOMESTIC COMMERCIAL SOFTWOODS

STANDARD LUMBER NAME	USDA FOREST SERVICE NAME	BOTANICAL NAME
Cedar, Alaska	Alaska Cedar	Chamaecyparis nootkatensis
Cedar, Eastern Red	Eastern Red Cedar	Juniperus virginiana
Cedar, Incense	Incense Cedar	Libocedrus decurrens
Cedar, Northern White	Northern White Cedar	Thuja occidentalis
Cedar, Port Orford	Port Orford Cedar	Chamaecyparis lawsoniana
Cedar, Southern White	Atlantic White Cedar	Chamaecyparis thyoides
Cedar, Western Red	Western Red Cedar	Thuja plicata
Cypress, Red (coast), Yellow (inland) and White (inland)	Bald Cypress	Taxodium distichum
Douglas Fir	Douglas Fir	Pseudotsuga menziesii
Fir, Balsam	Balsam Fir	Abies balsamea
Fir, Balsam	Fraser Fir	Abies fraseri
Fir, Noble	Noble Fir	Abies procera
Fir, White	California Red Fir	Abies magnifica
Fir, White	Grand Fir	Abies grandis
Fir, White	Pacific Silver Fir	Abies amabilis
Fir, White	Subalpine Fir	Abies lasiocarpa
Fir, White	White Fir	Abies concolor
Hemlock, Eastern	Eastern Hemlock	Tsuga canadensis
Hemlock, Mountain	Mountain Hemlock	Tsuga mertensiana
Hemlock, West Coast	Western Hemlock	Tsuga heterophylla
Juniper, Western	Alligator Juniper	Juniperus deppeana
Juniper, Western	Rocky Mountain Juniper	Juniperus scopulorum
Juniper, Western	Utah Juniper	Juniperus osteosperma
Juniper, Western	Western Juniper	Juniperus occidentalis
Larch, Western	Western Larch	Larix occidentalis
Pine, Idaho White	Western White Pine	Pinus monticola

STANDARD LUMBER NAME	USDA FOREST SERVICE NAME	BOTANICAL NAME
Pine, Jack	Jack Pine	Pinus banksiana
Pine, Lodgepole	Lodgepole Pine	Pinus contorta
Pine, Longleaf Yellow	Longleaf Pine	Pinus palustris
Pine, Longleaf Yellow	Slash Pine	Pinus elliottii
Pine, Northern White	Eastern White Pine	Pinus strobus
Pine, Norway	Red Pine	Pinus resinosa
Pine, Ponderosa	Ponderosa Pine	Pinus ponderosa
Pine, Southern	Longleaf Pine	Pinus palustris
Pine, Southern	Shortleaf Pine	Pinus echinata
Pine, Southern	Loblolly Pine	Pinus taeda
Pine, Southern	Slash Pine	Pinus elliottii
Pine, Southern	Pitch Pine	Pinus rigida
Pine, Southern	Pond Pine	Pinus serotina
Pine, Southern	Virginia Pine	Pinus virginiana
Pine, Sugar	Sugar Pine	Pinus lambertiana
Redwood	Redwood	Sequoia sempervirens
Spruce, Eastern	Black Spruce	Picea mariana
Spruce, Eastern	Red Spruce	Picea rubens
Spruce, Eastern	White Spruce	Picea glauca
Spruce, Engelmann	Blue Spruce	Picea pungens
Spruce, Engelmann	Engelmann Spruce	Picea engelmannii
Spruce, Sitka	Sitka Spruce	Picea sitchensis
Tamarack	Tamarack	Larix laricina
Yew, Pacific	Pacific Yew	Taxus brevifolia

COMMON AND BOTANICAL NAMES FOR SOME IMPORTED HARDWOODS

COMMON NAME	OTHER NAME(S)	BOTANICAL NAME(S)
Afara	Limba	Terminalia superba
African Mahogany	—	Khaya ivorensis, Khaya anthotheca
African Rosewood	Bubinga	Guibourtia spp.
African Whitewood	Obeche	Triplochiton scleroxylon
Afrormosia	Kokrodua	Pericopsis elata
Albarco	Jequitiba	Cariniana spp.
Amaranth	Purpleheart	Peltogyne spp.
Anani	Manni	Symphonia globulifera
Anaura	Kauta, Marishballi	Licania spp.
Andiroba	Crabwood	Carapa guianensis
Angelique	—	Dicorynia guianensis
Balsa	—	Ochroma pyramidale
Benge	—	Guibourtia arnoldiana
Bolivian Rosewood	—	Machaerium acutifolium
Brazilian Rosewood	Jacaranda	Dalbergia nigra
Bubinga	African Rosewood	Guibourtia spp.
Central American Mahogany	Honduras Mahogany, South American Mahogany	Swietenia macrophylla
Cocobolo	—	Dalbergia retusa
Crabwood	Andiroba	Carapa guianensis
Ebony	African Ebony, Ceylon Ebony, East Indian Ebony	Diospyros spp.
Goncalo Alves	—	Astronium spp.
Honduras Mahogany	Central American Mahogany, South American Mahogany	Swietenia macrophylla
Honduras Rosewood	—	Dalbergia stevensonii
Indian Rosewood	—	Dalbergia latifolia
Iroko	Kambala	Chlorophora excelsa, Chlorophora regia
Jacaranda	Brazilian Rosewood	Dalbergia nigra
Jarra	Red Ironwood	Eucalyptus marginata
Jequitiba	Albarco	Cariniana spp.
Kambala	Iroko	Chlorophora excelsa, Chlorophora regia

COMMON NAME	OTHER NAME(S)	BOTANICAL NAME(S)
Kauta	Anaura, Marishballi	Licania spp.
Kokrodua	Afrormosia	Pericopsis elata
Lacewood	Silky Oak	Cardwellia sublimis, Grevillea robusta
Lauan	Philippine Mahogany	Shorea spp., Parashorea spp., Pentacme spp.
Lignum Vitae	—	Guaiacum officinale, Guaiacum sanctum
Limba	Afara	Terminalia superba
Mahogany, African	—	Khaya ivorensis, Khaya anthotheca
Mahogany, Philippine	Lauan	Shorea spp., Parashorea spp., Pentacme spp.
Mahogany, South American	Central American Mahogany, Honduras Mahogany	Swietenia macrophylla
Manni	Anani	Symphonia globulifera
Marishballi	Anaura, Kauta	Licania spp.
Obeche	African Whitewood	Triplochiton scleroxylon
Philippine Mahogany	Lauan	Shorea spp. Parashorea spp., Pentacme spp.
Padauk	Vermillion	Pterocarpus soyauxii
Primavera	—	Cybistax donnellsmithii
Purpleheart	Amaranth	Peltogyne spp.
Ramin	—	Gonystylus bancanus
Red Ironwood	Jarra	Eucalyptus marginata
Rosewood, Bolivian	—	Machaerium acutifolium
Rosewood, Brazilian	Jacaranda	Dalbergia nigra
Rosewood, Honduras	—	Dalbergia stevensonii
Rosewood, Indian	—	Dalbergia latifolia
South American Mahogany	Central American Mahogany, Honduras Mahogany	Swietenia macrophylla
Teak	—	Tectona grandis
Vermillion	Padauk	Pterocarpus soyauxii
Wenge	—	Milletia spp.
Zebrawood	—	Microberlinia spp.

HOW TO CALCULATE BOARD FEET

The board foot is a measure of volume. One board foot is equal to 144 square inches or a board that measures 1" thick (nominal dimension) by 12" wide (nominal dimension) by 1' long (actual dimension).

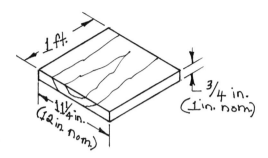

Several formulas can be used to calculate board feet, but the one most often used is as follows:

Board feet = thickness (inches) × width (inches) × length (feet)/12

To use the formula for any piece of lumber, multiply the thickness (in inches) by the width (in inches) by the length (in feet) and divide the resulting number by 12. Nominal dimensions *must* be used for the length and width.

Example: How many board feet are in a 10' length of 1 ×6" lumber?

1. Plug the numbers into the formula.

Board feet = 1 ×6 ×10/12

2. Multiply the thickness, width and length.

Board feet = 60/12

3. Divide by 12.

Board feet = 5

If you prefer to avoid math, the Board Footage Chart on page 76 lists board footages for a variety of board sizes and lengths.

BOARD FOOTAGE CHART

Use this chart to determine board footages for the most common nominal sizes and lumber lengths. The chart also includes a column that shows the number of board feet per linear foot for each nominal size. For sizes not shown, see How to Calculate Board Feet on page 75.

NOMINAL SIZE OF BOARD (inches)	BOARD FEET PER LINEAR FOOT	BOARD FEET (to nearest hundreth)					
		LENGTH OF BOARD (feet)					
		6	8	10	12	14	16
½×2	.0833	.50	.67	.83	1.00	1.17	1.33
½×3	.1250	.75	1.00	1.25	1.50	1.75	2.00
½×4	.1666	1.00	1.33	1.67	2.00	2.33	2.67
½×6	.2500	1.50	2.00	2.50	3.00	3.50	4.00
½×8	.3333	2.00	2.67	3.33	4.00	4.67	5.33
½×10	.4166	2.50	3.33	4.17	5.00	5.83	6.67
½×12	.5000	3.00	4.00	5.00	6.00	7.00	8.00
1×2	.1667	1.00	1.33	1.67	2.00	2.33	2.67
1×3	.2500	1.50	2.00	2.50	3.00	3.50	4.00
1×4	.3333	2.00	2.67	3.33	4.00	4.67	5.33
1×6	.5000	3.00	4.00	5.00	6.00	7.00	8.00
1×8	.6667	4.00	5.33	6.67	8.00	9.33	10.67
1×10	.8333	5.00	6.67	8.33	10.00	11.67	13.33
1×12	1.0000	6.00	8.00	10.00	12.00	14.00	16.00
2×2	.3333	2.00	2.67	3.33	4.00	4.67	5.33
2×3	.5000	3.00	4.00	5.00	6.00	7.00	8.00
2×4	.6667	4.00	5.33	6.67	8.00	9.33	10.67
2×6	1.0000	6.00	8.00	10.00	12.00	14.00	16.00
2×8	1.3333	8.00	10.67	13.33	16.00	18.67	21.33
2×10	1.6667	10.00	13.33	16.67	20.00	23.33	26.67
2×12	2.0000	12.00	16.00	20.00	24.00	28.00	32.00
2×14	2.3333	14.00	18.67	23.33	28.00	32.67	37.33
3×3	.7500	4.50	6.00	7.50	9.00	10.50	12.00
3×4	1.0000	6.00	8.00	10.00	12.00	14.00	16.00
3×6	1.5000	9.00	12.00	15.00	18.00	21.00	24.00
3×8	2.0000	12.00	16.00	20.00	24.00	28.00	32.00
3×10	2.5000	15.00	20.00	25.00	30.00	35.00	40.00
3×12	3.0000	18.00	24.00	30.00	36.00	42.00	48.00
3×14	3.5000	21.00	28.00	35.00	42.00	49.00	56.00
3×16	4.0000	24.00	32.00	40.00	48.00	56.00	64.00
4×4	1.3333	8.00	10.67	13.33	16.00	18.67	21.33
4×6	2.0000	12.00	16.00	20.00	24.00	28.00	32.00
4×8	2.6667	16.00	21.33	26.67	32.00	37.33	42.67
4×10	3.3333	20.00	26.67	33.33	40.00	46.67	53.33
4×12	4.0000	24.00	32.00	40.00	48.00	56.00	64.00
6×6	3.0000	18.00	24.00	30.00	36.00	42.00	48.00
6×8	4.0000	24.00	32.00	40.00	48.00	56.00	64.00
6×10	5.0000	30.00	40.00	50.00	60.00	70.00	80.00
6×12	6.0000	36.00	48.00	60.00	72.00	84.00	96.00

SOFTWOOD LUMBER GRADES

Softwood lumber that's used as structural members (studs, joists, rafters and the like) is classified as framing lumber. Lumber to be used for appearance applications (paneling, molding, shelving, furniture) is classified as appearance lumber.

Framing lumber is graded primarily on the strength characteristics of the wood, with appearance a secondary consideration. Appearance lumber is graded to meet appearance standards first, and in most cases strength standards are not considered.

Framing lumber has two broad classifications: dimension lumber and timbers. Most structural softwood lumber used for general building construction falls into either the dimension lumber or timber classifications.

DIMENSION LUMBER

Dimension lumber measures between 2″ and 4″ in nominal thickness and has nominal widths of 2″ or greater. It is used for framing members such as joists, planks, rafters, studs, posts and beams.

Light Framing Category

This is the most widely used category of lumber for framing houses. It is used when high-strength values are not required, such as wall framing, plates, blocking, sills and cripples. All lumber in this category has nominal widths of 2″ to 4″.

- Construction (Const): Highest grade in this category. Widely used for general framing applications.
- Standard (Stand): Used for same application as construction grade but is a bit less desirable. It may have more knots and somewhat less strength. Most building codes require that lumber used in house construction be standard grade or better.
- Utility (Util): Can be used for temporary bracing or blocking between studs and joists. Generally quite knotty. Check building codes for acceptance.

Structural Light Framing Category

These grades fit engineering applications where the highest strength is needed for uses such as trusses and concrete forms. All lumber in this category has nominal widths of 2″ to 4″.

- Select Structural (Sel Str): The highest grade in this category. This grade is used when both strength and appearance are important considerations.
- No. 1 (1): Used when good strength and appearance are required.
- No. 2 (2): This grade has a less pleasing appearance but still retains high strength. It is recommended for most general construction uses.
- No. 3 (3): Used for general construction when high strength isn't necessary.

Structural Joists and Planks Category

These grades fit engineering applications where higher strength is needed for such uses as trusses, joists, rafters and general framing. This category is graded according to the same guidelines that are used for the structural light framing category. All lumber in this category measures 5″ nominal and wider.

- Select Structural (Sel Str): The highest grade in this category. Used where both strength and appearance are the most important considerations.
- No. 1 (1): Used when both good strength and appearance are required.
- No. 2 (2): This grade has a less pleasing appearance but still retains high strength.
- No. 3 (3): Used for general construction when high strength isn't necessary.

Stud Category
A popular grade for load-bearing and non-load-bearing walls. All lumber in this grade measures 2″ nominal and wider.

- Stud: Specially selected for use as studs in house framing.

Note: All four categories also have an "Economy" grade (abbreviation: Econ). However, economy grade is not intended for structural applications.

TIMBERS
This is a general classification for the larger sizes of structural framing lumber, but it is also the name of a specific grade and size.

Beams and Stringers Category
Lumber in this category has nominal thicknesses of 5″ or more and widths more than 2″ greater than the thickness (6″×10″ or 8″×12″, for example).

- Select Structural (Sel Str): Selected primarily for strength properties, but most pieces also offer good appearance for exposed applications.
- No. 1 (1): This grade has good strength qualities and many pieces have a fine appearance.
- No. 2 (2): Used when serviceability is important but where higher strength properties are not required.
- No. 3 (3): Used when higher grade requirements are not required.

Posts and Timbers Category
This lumber has nominal dimensions of 5″×5″ and larger, and widths not more than 2″ greater than the thickness (6″×6″ or 8″×10″, for example).

- Select Structural (Sel Str): Selected primarily for strength properties, but most pieces also offer good appearance for exposed applications.
- No. 1 (1): This grade has good strength qualities and many pieces have a fine appearance.
- No. 2 (2): Used when serviceability is important but where higher strength properties are not required.
- No. 3 (3): Used when higher grade requirements are not required.

APPEARANCE LUMBER

Appearance lumber is often called board lumber or boards. It is graded primarily for appearance rather than strength. Boards can measure from ⅜" to 4" in thickness and have widths that are 2" nominal and greater. However, the appearance boards that you find in most building supply centers are likely to have 1" or 1¼" nominal thicknesses.

Select Grade Category

Select grades are used when the best appearance is required. The boards are graded from the best face. Select grades have a moisture content of 15 percent or less. The boards measure from 1" to 4" nominal thickness and have widths that are 2" nominal or greater. In the select grade category, grade names for Idaho white pine differ from those used for other species.

- B and Better Select (B & Btr Sel), or Supreme (Supreme) for Idaho white pine: This is the highest grade of select lumber. The boards might contain some small knots and slight blemishes, but many pieces are absolutely clear.
- C Select (C Sel), or Choice (Choice) for Idaho white pine: Slightly larger knots and more blemishes than B and better select, but is still a good quality lumber for cabinetwork.
- D Select (D Sel), or Quality (Quality) for Idaho white pine: Contains increasingly larger knots and knotholes, but it has many of the fine appearance features of the C select grade. It is often used as a backing or in areas that are not highly visible.

Finish Grade Category

Finish grade, like select grade, is used when the best appearance is required. It is picked from the best side and both edges of 5" nominal and narrower pieces and from the best side and one edge of 6" nominal and wider pieces. Finish grades measure from ⅜" to 4" nominal thickness and have widths that are 2" nominal or greater. The boards are dried to a moisture content of 15 percent or less.

- Superior Finish (Superior): This is the highest grade of the finish grades. Many pieces are clear.
- Prime Finish (Prime): This grade has a fine appearance, but it has slightly more defects than superior grade.
- E Finish (E): The E finish grade has more defects than the prime finish grade. This grade is often used when it is possible to rip or crosscut the lumber to remove the defects, resulting in material that is equivalent to prime or superior finish grades.

COMMON GRADE CATEGORY

Lumber in this category has more knots than those in the select and finish grades. Common grades measure from ¾″ to 4″ nominal thickness and have widths that are 2″ nominal and greater. In the common grade category, grade names for Idaho white pine differ from those used for other species.

- No. 1 (1 Com), or Colonial for Idaho white pine: No. 1 common grade has the best appearance of all the common grades. The knots are tight and relatively small.
- No. 2 (2 Com), or Sterling for Idaho white pine: This grade is used when a knotty material with a fine appearance is required. It is often used for paneling, shelving and cabinetwork. Also, since the knots can be sealed, the boards can be painted and used for siding, soffits, fascias, cornices and other exterior applications.
- No. 3 (3 Com), or Standard for Idaho white pine: Siding, paneling, shelving, sheathing, crating, fences and boxes are some of the uses for this grade.
- No. 4 (4 Com), or Utility for Idaho white pine: Boards in this grade are generally used for subfloors, wall and roof sheathing, concrete forms, crating and low-cost fencing.
- No. 5 (5 Com), or Industrial for Idaho white pine: This grade is used when appearance and strength are not important factors. The boards can include unsound wood, stains, massed pitch, large knots and holes, and heavy shakes, splits and wane.

ALTERNATE BOARD GRADES CATEGORY

Some mills manufacture boards to the grading standards in this category. The grades are determined using the best face of the board. Alternate board grades measure from ¾″ to 1½″ nominal thickness and have widths that are 2″ or greater.

- Select Merchantable (Sel Merch): This grade is used when knotty material can provide an acceptable appearance. Its uses include paneling and shelving.
- Construction (Const): Construction grade boards are used for roof and wall sheathing, subflooring, concrete forms and similar applications.
- Standard (Stand): This lumber is graded primarily on serviceability, although appearance is given some consideration. Lumber in this grade is usually used where it is not going to be exposed.
- Utility (Util): Utility grade lumber is selected for its utility values rather than appearance.
- Economy (Econ): The lowest grade in this category. It is often used for temporary construction. Economy grade is also used for low-grade sheathing, bracing, crating and similar applications.

Note: The grade names shown are based on the grading rules of the Western Wood Products Association. Grade names and specifications can sometimes vary among lumber grading agencies.

SOFTWOOD LUMBER STANDARD SIZES
(NOMINAL AND DRESSED; BASED ON WESTERN
WOOD PRODUCTS ASSOCIATION GRADING RULES)

Abbreviations:
S1S: Surfaced one side   S1S1E: Surfaced one side, one edge
S2S: Surfaced two sides   S1S2E: Surfaced one side, two edges
S4S: Surfaced four sides   Rough: Unsurfaced lumber cut to full specified size

FRAMING LUMBER—DIMENSION
S4S

NOMINAL SIZE		DRESSED DIMENSIONS THICKNESSES AND WIDTHS (inches)	
Thickness (inches)	Width (inches)	Surfaced Dry	Surfaced Unseasoned
2	2	$1\frac{1}{2}$	$1\frac{9}{16}$
3	3	$2\frac{1}{2}$	$2\frac{9}{16}$
4	4	$3\frac{1}{2}$	$3\frac{9}{16}$
	5	$4\frac{1}{2}$	$4\frac{5}{8}$
	6	$5\frac{1}{2}$	$5\frac{5}{8}$
	8	$7\frac{1}{4}$	$7\frac{1}{2}$
	10	$9\frac{1}{4}$	$9\frac{1}{2}$
	12	$11\frac{1}{4}$	$11\frac{1}{2}$
	over 12	off $\frac{3}{4}$	off $\frac{1}{2}$

FRAMING LUMBER—TIMBERS
Rough or S4S (shipped unseasoned)

NOMINAL SIZE (inches)	DIMENSIONS (unseasoned)
5 and larger	$\frac{1}{2}$ off nominal (S4S)

APPEARANCE LUMBER—SELECTS AND COMMONS

S1S, S2S, S4S, S1S1E, S1S2E

NOMINAL SIZE		DRY DRESSED DIMENSIONS	
Thickness (inches)	Width (inches)	Thickness (inches)	Width (inches)
4/4	2	$3/4$	$1\frac{1}{2}$
5/4	3	$1\frac{5}{32}$	$2\frac{1}{2}$
6/4	4	$1\frac{13}{32}$	$3\frac{1}{2}$
7/4	5	$1\frac{19}{32}$	$4\frac{1}{2}$
8/4	6	$1\frac{13}{16}$	$5\frac{1}{2}$
9/4	7	$2\frac{3}{32}$	$6\frac{1}{2}$
10/4	8 and wider	$2\frac{3}{8}$	$3/4$ off nominal
11/4		$2\frac{9}{16}$	
12/4		$2\frac{3}{4}$	
16/4		$3\frac{3}{4}$	

APPEARANCE LUMBER—FINISH AND ALTERNATE BOARD GRADES

*Only these sizes apply to alternate board grades.

NOMINAL SIZE		DRY DRESSED DIMENSIONS	
Thickness (inches)	Width (inches)	Thickness (inches)	Width (inches)
$3/8$	2	$5/16$	$1\frac{1}{2}$
$1/2$	3	$7/16$	$2\frac{1}{2}$
$5/8$	4	$9/16$	$3\frac{1}{2}$
*$3/4$	5	$5/8$	$4\frac{1}{2}$
*1	6	$3/4$	$5\frac{1}{2}$
*$1\frac{1}{4}$	7	1	$6\frac{1}{2}$
*$1\frac{1}{2}$	8 and wider	$1\frac{1}{4}$	$3/4$ off nominal
$1\frac{3}{4}$		$1\frac{3}{8}$	
2		$1\frac{1}{2}$	
$2\frac{1}{2}$		2	
3		$2\frac{1}{2}$	
$3\frac{1}{2}$		3	
4		$3\frac{1}{2}$	

TYPICAL SOFTWOOD LUMBER GRADE STAMP

Most grading stamps, except those for rough lumber or heavy timbers, contain five basic elements:

1. Grade designation. Shows grade name, number or abbreviation.
2. Species identification mark. Indicates species by individual species or species combination. Shown below are some of the marks of the Western Wood Products Association.
3. Condition of seasoning. Indicates condition of seasoning at time of surfacing.
   MC-15: 15 percent maximum moisture content
   S-DRY: 19 percent maximum moisture content
   S-GRN: over 19 percent moisture content (unseasoned)
4. Official certification mark of the lumber association. Shown is the mark of the Western Wood Products Association.
5. Mill identification. Shows firm name, brand name or assigned mill number.

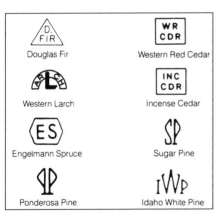

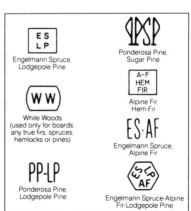

Some WWPA grade stamps identify an individual Western lumber species.

Because of timber stand composition, some mills market additional species combinations.

EXAMPLES OF SOFTWOOD LUMBER GRADE STAMPS

Grade stamp examples courtesy Western Wood Products Association.

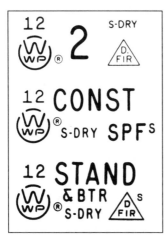

Dimension Grades

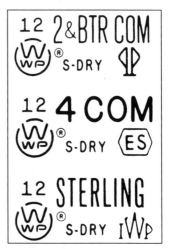

Commons

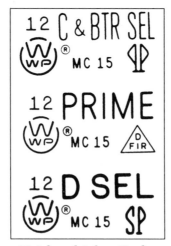

Finish and Select Grades

PRESSURE-TREATED LUMBER RETENTION LEVELS

Wood exposed to moisture for long periods of time provides a perfect breeding ground for fungi to grow, and that usually results in wood decay. Also, wood is subject to attack by wood-boring insects that can weaken the structure. Wood that is pressure-treated enjoys an excellent defense against damage from decay and insects. Standards for pressure-treated wood have been developed by the American Wood Preservers' Institute (AWPI).

Wood preservatives fall into three broad classes: creosote, oil-borne, and waterborne. Unlike creosote and oil-borne preservatives, waterborne preservatives (which use water as the solvent) leave the wood surfaces relatively clean, odor-free and paintable. Therefore, most of the pressure-treated wood sold for residential construction incorporates the waterborne preservatives. Indeed, countless backyard decks are now made from wood treated with a waterborne preservative.

Chromated copper arsenate (CCA) and ammoniacal copper zinc arsenate (ACZA) are the most commonly used waterborne preservatives. Both of these preservatives contain inorganic arsenic, so it makes good sense to follow some basic safety measures when working with pressure-treated wood. See Working With Pressure-Treated Wood on page 184 for specific safety information.

The pressure-treating process forces the waterborne preservative deep into the wood. Resistance to fungus growth and insect attack is directly related to the amount of chemical that is added to the wood. The chemical retention level is shown as the number of pounds of chemical retained per cubic foot (pcf) of wood. A higher retention level indicates a higher resistance to fungus and insect attack.

RETENTION LEVEL (pounds pcf)	EXPOSURE CONDITIONS	TYPICAL APPLICATIONS
.25	Above ground	Outdoor deck parts not in contact with the ground
.40	Contact with soil or fresh water	Landscape timbers
.60	Below ground	Wood foundations, sign posts
1.00	Immersion in fresh water	Freshwater piling
2.50	Immersion in salt water	Saltwater piling

TYPICAL QUALITY MARK FOR PRESSURE-TREATED LUMBER

Manufacturers associated with the American Wood Preservers' Institute (AWPI) apply a quality mark to pressure-treated lumber, either in the form of an ink stamp or an end tag. The mark provides a variety of useful information about the pressure-treated wood. Sample below courtesy of American Wood Preservers Institute, Vienna, Virginia.

1. Year of treatment
2. Preservative used for treatment
3. Proper exposure conditions
4. Retention level
5. Trademark of the inspection agency
6. Applicable AWPI standard
7. Treating company and location

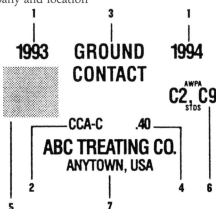

HARDWOOD LUMBER GRADES
(GENERAL REQUIREMENTS FOR EACH GRADE)

Hardwood lumber is graded differently than softwood lumber. The grading rules for hardwood lumber are established by the National Hardwood Lumber Association (NHLA).

Basically, each hardwood board is graded based on the number and size of usable pieces of wood (called cuttings) that can be obtained from a board once any defects are cut out. That means, in effect, that after cutting away the defects in a *high-grade* board, you'll have a low percentage of waste and end up with a relatively small number of large-sized boards. And, after cutting away the defects in a *low-grade* board, you'll have a higher percentage of waste and a relatively large number of small-sized boards. Grades are usually determined using the poorest side of the board.

In most cases, a cutting must be "clear-faced" on at least one side in order to be considered usable. Some lower grades accept "sound cuttings," which can have several types of imperfections including stains, streaks, bird pecks, sound knots and some small holes.

The grades shown in the chart are sometimes combined. For example, grades FAS, F1F and Selects might be combined and sold as grade "Select and Better." Grades 2A common and 2B common are often combined and sold as grade number 2 Common. In some regions, grades FAS and Selects are substituted for one another.

Not surprisingly, higher grades are more expensive than lower grades. However, the best grade to use depends on how you plan to use the wood. For example, if you must have long, clear-cut boards for the side of a tall cupboard, you are going to need the select grade, or perhaps even FAS. That's because those grades, as dictated by the NHLA rules, have the longest clear-cut boards. However, if you need relatively short, narrow pieces for a chair, you might find that number 1 common grade is the more economical way to go.

Finally, and perhaps most importantly, there is no substitute for your own eyes. Try to examine any lumber before you buy. Usually, a quick inspection will tell you if a board can provide the stock you need.

The following chart shows the general requirements for the standard grades. For detailed information, refer to the NHLA rulebook. It can be ordered from the National Hardwood Lumber Association, P.O. Box 34518, Memphis, TN 38184-0518.

HARDWOOD LUMBER GRADE	MINIMUM BOARD SIZE	MINIMUM SIZE CUTTING	BASIC YIELD (percentage)	MAX. NUMBER OF CLEAR-FACED CUTTINGS
FAS (first and seconds)	6"×8'	4"×5' or 3"×7'	83⅓	4
F1F (first and seconds, one face)	6"×8'	4"×5' or 3"×7'	83⅓	4
Selects	4"×6'	4"×5' or 3"×7'	83⅓	4
No. 1 Common	3"×4'	4"×2' or 3"×3'	66⅔	5
No. 2A Common	3"×4'	3"×2'	50	7
No. 2B Common	3"×4'	3"×2'	50	7 sound cuttings
No. 3A Common	3"×4'	3"×2'	33⅓	Unlimited
No. 3B Common	3"×4'	Not less than 1½" wide containing 36 square inches	25	Unlimited sound cuttings

Note: Chart applies to most, but not all, hardwood species. See NHLA rulebook for exceptions.

STANDARD THICKNESSES FOR HARDWOOD LUMBER (ROUGH AND SURFACED)

ROUGH (inches)	S2S (surfaced two sides) (inches)	ROUGH (inches)	S2S (surfaced two sides) (inches)
3/8	3/16	2½	2¼
½	5/16	3	2¾
5/8	7/16	3½	3¼
¾	9/16	4	3¾
1	13/16	4½	–
1¼	1 1/16	5	–
1½	1 5/16	5½	–
1¾	1½	6	–
2	1¾		

RECOMMENDED AVERAGE MOISTURE CONTENT

(FOR WOOD USED TO MAKE INTERIOR FURNITURE)

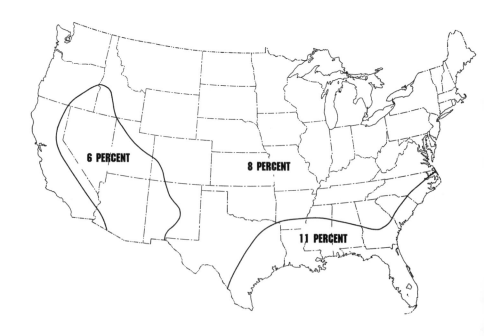

HOW TO DETERMINE WOOD MOISTURE CONTENT

A moisture meter is the fastest and easiest way to measure the moisture content in a piece of wood. Although moisture meters have become more affordable in recent years, most woodworkers feel the cost is still too high to justify the expense.

Without a moisture meter in hand, your best option is to calculate the moisture content. Although the procedure is quite accurate, it isn't altogether practical for the average hobbyist woodworker. That's because you need a laboratory (gram) scale or an equivalent scale to get accurate weight measurements of the wood sample. Then, too, it can take up to twenty-four hours for the sample to fully dry in a kitchen oven—a procedure that's likely to disrupt the kitchen cooking schedule.

To do the test, you'll need a wood sample that's about 1" thick by 3" wide by 1" long. Cutting the sample in this manner exposes a considerable amount of end grain, which helps the sample dry faster. Check to make sure that the sample doesn't have any knots or other defects. Also, avoid cutting the sample from the ends, as that area tends to be drier than other parts of the board.

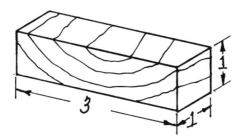

Weigh the sample using the laboratory scale and note the weight. Then, place the sample in the oven and bake it at a temperature of 210° to 220° Fahrenheit. Re-weigh the sample about every eight hours, taking care to avoid scorching the wood as it dries. When the sample no longer loses weight, it is at the oven-dry weight, which means it is completely free of water and has a moisture content of zero. Once you have the oven-dry weight of the sample, you can determine the wood moisture content (MC) by using the following formula:

$$MC = (\text{Original weight} - \text{Oven-dry weight})/(\text{Oven-dry weight}) \times 100$$

Example
The original weight of a sample is 14 grams. After completely drying in the oven, the sample weighs 12 grams. The moisture content of the sample was:

$$MC = (14 \text{ grams} - 12 \text{ grams})/(12 \text{ grams}) \times 100$$
$$= 2 \text{ grams}/12 \text{ grams} \times 100$$
$$= .167 \times 100$$
$$= 16.7 \text{ percent}$$

EQUILIBRIUM MOISTURE CONTENT

Wood either gains or loses moisture in an effort to be in balance with the relative humidity of the surrounding air. Place a dry board in a damp basement and the wood starts to slowly absorb moisture. If, after a few months, you move the same board into a bone-dry living room, the wood will start to dry out.

The amount of water in wood, expressed as a percentage of its oven-dry weight, is called its *moisture content*. (See page 89, How to Determine Wood Moisture Content.) The *equilibrium moisture content* (EMC) is defined as that moisture content at which wood is neither gaining nor losing moisture. Both temperature and relative humidity affect the EMC. The chart that follows shows the EMC for a wide range of temperature and relative humidity values.

TEMP. (° F)	EQUILIBRIUM MOISTURE CONTENT (PERCENT) AT A RELATIVE HUMIDITY OF:									
	5%	10%	15%	20%	25%	30%	35%	40%	45%	50%
30	1.4	2.6	3.7	4.6	5.5	6.3	7.1	7.9	8.7	9.5
40	1.4	2.6	3.7	4.6	5.5	6.3	7.1	7.9	8.7	9.5
50	1.4	2.6	3.6	4.6	5.5	6.3	7.1	7.9	8.7	9.5
60	1.3	2.5	3.6	4.6	5.4	6.2	7.0	7.8	8.6	9.4
70	1.3	2.5	3.5	4.5	5.4	6.2	6.9	7.7	8.5	9.2
80	1.3	2.4	3.5	4.4	5.3	6.1	6.8	7.6	8.3	9.1
90	1.2	2.3	3.4	4.3	5.1	5.9	6.7	7.4	8.1	8.9
100	1.2	2.3	3.3	4.2	5.0	5.8	6.5	7.2	7.9	8.7
110	1.1	2.2	3.2	4.0	4.9	5.6	6.3	7.0	7.7	8.4
120	1.1	2.1	3.0	3.9	4.7	5.4	6.1	6.8	7.5	8.2
130	1.0	2.0	2.9	3.7	4.5	5.2	5.9	6.6	7.2	7.9
140	.9	1.9	2.8	3.6	4.3	5.0	5.7	6.3	7.0	7.7
150	.9	1.8	2.6	3.4	4.1	4.8	5.5	6.1	6.7	7.4
160	.8	1.6	2.4	3.2	3.9	4.6	5.2	5.8	6.4	7.1
170	.7	1.5	2.3	3.0	3.7	4.3	4.9	5.6	6.2	6.8
180	.7	1.4	2.1	2.8	3.5	4.1	4.7	5.3	5.9	6.5
190	.6	1.3	1.9	2.6	3.2	3.8	4.4	5.0	5.5	6.1
200	.5	1.1	1.7	2.4	3.0	3.5	4.1	4.6	5.2	5.8
210	.5	1.0	1.6	2.1	2.7	3.2	3.8	4.3	4.9	5.4
220	.4	.9	1.4	1.9	2.4	2.9	3.4	3.9	4.5	5.0
230	.3	.8	1.2	1.6	2.1	2.6	3.1	3.6	4.2	4.7
240	.3	.6	.9	1.3	1.7	2.1	2.6	3.1	3.5	4.1
250	.2	.4	.7	1.0	1.3	1.7	2.1	2.5	2.9	*

TEMP. (° F)	EQUILIBRIUM MOISTURE CONTENT (PERCENT) AT A RELATIVE HUMIDITY OF:									
	55%	60%	65%	70%	75%	80%	85%	90%	95%	98%
30	10.4	11.3	12.4	13.5	14.9	16.5	18.5	21.0	24.3	26.9
40	10.4	11.3	12.3	13.5	14.9	16.5	18.5	21.0	24.3	26.9
50	10.3	11.2	12.3	13.4	14.8	16.4	18.4	20.9	24.3	26.9
60	10.2	11.1	12.1	13.3	14.6	16.2	18.2	20.7	24.1	26.8
70	10.1	11.0	12.0	13.1	14.4	16.0	17.9	20.5	23.9	26.6
80	9.9	10.8	11.7	12.9	14.2	15.7	17.7	20.2	23.6	26.3
90	9.7	10.5	11.5	12.6	13.9	15.4	17.3	19.8	23.3	26.0
100	9.5	10.3	11.2	12.3	13.6	15.1	17.0	19.5	22.9	25.6
110	9.2	10.0	11.0	12.0	13.2	14.7	16.6	19.1	22.4	25.2
120	8.9	9.7	10.6	11.7	12.9	14.4	16.2	18.6	22.0	24.7
130	8.7	9.4	10.3	11.3	12.5	14.0	15.8	18.2	21.5	24.2
140	8.4	9.1	10.0	11.0	12.1	13.6	15.3	17.7	21.0	23.7
150	8.1	8.8	9.7	10.6	11.8	13.1	14.9	17.2	20.4	23.1
160	7.8	8.5	9.3	10.3	11.4	12.7	14.4	16.7	19.9	22.5
170	7.4	8.2	9.0	9.9	11.0	12.3	14.0	16.2	19.3	21.9
180	7.1	7.8	8.6	9.5	10.5	11.8	13.5	15.7	18.7	21.3
190	6.8	7.5	8.2	9.1	10.1	11.4	13.0	15.1	18.1	20.7
200	6.4	7.1	7.8	8.7	9.7	10.9	12.5	14.6	17.5	20.0
210	6.0	6.7	7.4	8.3	9.2	10.4	12.0	14.0	16.9	19.3
220	5.6	6.3	7.0	7.8	8.8	9.9	*	*	*	*
230	5.3	6.0	6.7	*	*	*	*	*	*	*
240	4.6	*	*	*	*	*	*	*	*	*
250	*	*	*	*	*	*	*	*	*	*

* Conditions not possible at atmospheric pressure.

WOODSHOP APPLICATION

Using the Equilibrium Moisture Content Table on Page 90–91

A basement woodshop in the northeastern United States has a year-round temperature of 60° and an constant relative humidity (with the help of a dehumidifier) of 50 percent.

1. What is the moisture content of the lumber stored for long periods of time in the basement? Referring to the table, it can be seen that the wood has an EMC of 9.4 percent at 60° Fahrenheit and 50 percent relative humidity. In short, that means lumber stored in the basement for a long enough period of time is going to end up with a moisture content of 9.4 percent.

2. Is the lumber dry enough to be used for furniture making? Referring to Recommended Average Moisture Content (page 88), it can be seen that in the northeastern United States, the average moisture content should be 8 percent. At 9.4 percent, the lumber isn't dry enough to use for furniture.

Again using the EMC table, it can be seen that the lumber can eventually be dried to 7.8 percent moisture content, an acceptable level, by maintaining the same temperature while lowering the relative humidity to 40 percent.

WOOD SHRINKAGE

When a tree is harvested, the water in the cells starts to evaporate and the wood slowly dries. Little dimensional change occurs until the wood reaches its *fiber saturation point*. For most woods, the fiber saturation point is about 30 percent moisture content, although that number can vary up to several percentage points. Wood with a moisture content higher than the fiber saturation point is called *green wood*.

As the moisture content falls below the fiber saturation point, the wood begins to shrink primarily in two directions. Tangential shrinkage occurs in the same direction as the annular rings, while radial shrinkage occurs in a direction perpendicular to the annular rings. Little shrinkage occurs in the longitudinal direction, which is parallel to the grain of the wood. Indeed, the amount of longitudinal shrinkage is considered negligible for most woodworking projects.

The chart on the next four pages shows the amount of radial and tangential shrinkage (from green to oven-dry) for a number of domestic hardwoods, domestic softwoods and imported woods. The chart is useful in a general way because it shows that, for all wood species, tangential shrinkage is considerably more than radial shrinkage (about twice as much on average).

The chart also allows you to quickly compare the shrinkage value of one wood species to another. For example, if you must keep wood movement to a minimum and you have the option of using black cherry or sugar maple, the chart quickly shows that black cherry is the better choice.

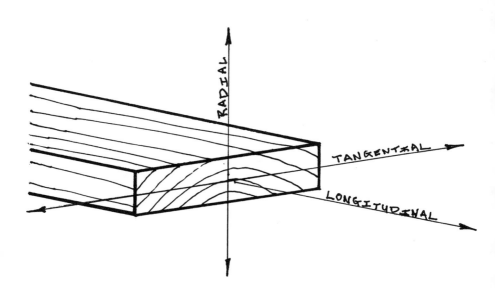

SHRINKAGE VALUES OF VARIOUS WOOD SPECIES

SPECIES	SHRINKAGE (IN PERCENT) FROM GREEN TO OVEN-DRY MOISTURE CONTENT	
	Radial	Tangential
Domestic Hardwoods		
Alder, Red	4.4	7.3
Ash, Black	5.0	7.8
Ash, Blue	3.9	6.5
Ash, Green	4.6	7.1
Ash, Oregon	4.1	8.1
Ash, Pumpkin	3.7	6.3
Ash, White	4.9	7.8
Aspen, Bigtooth	3.3	7.9
Aspen, Quaking	3.5	6.7
Basswood, American	6.6	9.3
Beech, American	5.5	11.9
Birch, Alaska Paper	6.5	9.9
Birch, Gray	5.2	–
Birch, Paper	6.3	8.6
Birch, River	4.7	9.2
Birch, Sweet	6.5	9.0
Birch, Yellow	7.3	9.5
Buckeye, Yellow	3.6	8.1
Butternut	3.4	6.4
Cherry, Black	3.7	7.1
Chestnut, American	3.4	6.7
Cottonwood, Balsam Poplar	3.0	7.1
Cottonwood, Black	3.6	8.6
Cottonwood, Eastern	3.9	9.2
Elm, American	4.2	9.5
Elm, Cedar	4.7	10.2
Elm, Rock	4.8	8.1
Elm, Slippery	4.9	8.9
Elm, Winged	5.3	11.6
Hackberry	4.8	8.9
Hickory, Pecan	4.9	8.9
Hickory (True), Mockernut	7.7	11.0
Hickory (True), Pignut	7.2	11.5
Hickory (True), Shagbark	7.0	10.5
Hickory (True), Shellbark	7.6	12.6
Holly, American	4.8	9.9

SPECIES	SHRINKAGE (IN PERCENT) FROM GREEN TO OVEN-DRY MOISTURE CONTENT	
	Radial	Tangential
Honey Locust	4.2	6.6
Locust, Black	4.6	7.2
Madrone, Pacific	5.6	12.4
Magnolia, Cucumber Tree	5.2	8.8
Magnolia, Southern	5.4	6.6
Magnolia, Sweet Bay	4.7	8.3
Maple, Bigleaf	3.7	7.1
Maple, Black	4.8	9.3
Maple, Red	4.0	8.2
Maple, Silver	3.0	7.2
Maple, Striped	3.2	8.6
Maple, Sugar	4.8	9.9
Oak (Red), Black	4.4	11.1
Oak (Red), Laurel	4.0	9.9
Oak (Red), Northern Red	4.0	8.6
Oak (Red), Pin	4.3	9.5
Oak (Red), Scarlet	4.4	10.8
Oak (Red), Southern Red	4.7	11.3
Oak (Red), Water	4.4	9.8
Oak (Red), Willow	5.0	9.6
Oak (White), Burr	4.4	8.8
Oak (White), Chestnut	5.3	10.8
Oak (White), Live	6.6	9.5
Oak (White), Overcup	5.3	12.7
Oak (White), Post	5.4	9.8
Oak (White), Swamp Chestnut	5.2	10.8
Oak, White	5.6	10.5
Persimmon, Common	7.9	11.2
Sassafras	4.0	6.2
Sweet Gum	5.3	10.2
Sycamore, American	5.0	8.4
Tan Oak	4.9	11.7
Tupelo, Black	5.1	8.7
Tupelo, Water	4.2	7.6
Walnut, Black	5.5	7.8
Willow, Black	3.3	8.7
Yellow Poplar	4.6	8.2

SPECIES	SHRINKAGE (IN PERCENT) FROM GREEN TO OVEN-DRY MOISTURE CONTENT	
	Radial	Tangential
Domestic Softwoods		
Bald Cypress	3.8	6.2
Cedar, Alaska	2.8	6.0
Cedar, Atlantic White	2.9	5.4
Cedar, Eastern Red	3.1	4.7
Cedar, Incense	3.3	5.2
Cedar, Northern White	2.2	4.9
Cedar, Port Orford	4.6	6.9
Cedar, Western Red	2.4	5.0
Douglas Fir, Coast	4.8	7.6
Douglas Fir, Interior North	3.8	6.9
Douglas Fir, Interior West	4.8	7.5
Fir, Balsam	2.9	6.9
Fir, California Red	4.5	7.9
Fir, Grand	3.4	7.5
Fir, Noble	4.3	8.3
Fir, Pacific Silver	4.4	9.2
Fir, Subalpine	2.6	7.4
Fir, White	3.3	7.0
Hemlock, Eastern	3.0	6.8
Hemlock, Mountain	4.4	7.1
Hemlock, Western	4.2	7.8
Larch, Western	4.5	9.1
Pine, Eastern White	2.1	6.1
Pine, Jack	3.7	6.6
Pine, Loblolly	4.8	7.4
Pine, Lodgepole	4.3	6.7
Pine, Longleaf	5.1	7.5
Pine, Pitch	4.0	7.1
Pine, Pond	5.1	7.1
Pine, Ponderosa	3.9	6.2
Pine, Red	3.8	7.2
Pine, Shortleaf	4.6	7.7
Pine, Slash	5.4	7.6
Pine, Sugar	2.9	5.6
Pine, Virginia	4.2	7.2
Pine, Western White	4.1	7.4

SPECIES	SHRINKAGE (IN PERCENT) FROM GREEN TO OVEN-DRY MOISTURE CONTENT	
	Radial	Tangential
Redwood, old-growth	2.6	4.4
Redwood, young-growth	2.2	4.9
Spruce, Black	4.1	6.8
Spruce, Engelmann	3.8	7.1
Spruce, Red	3.8	7.8
Spruce, Sitka	4.3	7.5
Tamarack	3.7	7.4
Some Imported Woods		
Afrormosia	3.0	6.4
Balsa	3.0	7.6
Benge	5.2	8.6
Bubinga	5.8	8.4
Ebony	5.5	6.5
Lauan (Shorea spp.)	3.8	8.0
Mahogany, African	2.5	4.5
Mahogany, Honduras	3.0	4.1
Purpleheart	3.2	6.1
Rosewood, Brazilian	2.9	4.6
Rosewood, Indian	2.7	5.8
Teak	2.5	5.8

TIME REQUIRED TO AIR-DRY LUMBER TO 20 PERCENT MOISTURE CONTENT

Shown on the next two pages are the approximate number of days required to air-dry 1″-thick green lumber to a moisture content of 20 percent. To provide the best opportunity for drying, the lumber should be stickered to allow air circulation between the boards.

You'll note that the drying time for each species varies considerably. That's because, to a large extent, the drying time depends upon the season of the year that the lumber is set out to dry. For example, the drying time for lumber set out in the spring and summer, which are the best months for drying, is likely to be near the minimum number of days. But lumber set out to dry in the fall or winter isn't likely to reach 20 percent moisture content until the following spring.

The drying times should be considered as rough approximations because average drying conditions can vary considerably from one year to the next. For example, an unusually cool, damp spring is going to lengthen the drying time for that season. Also, keep in mind that lumber at 20 percent moisture content must be further dried before it can be used for furniture (see page 88, Recommended Average Moisture Content).

DRYING TIME—HARDWOODS

SPECIES	DAYS REQUIRED TO AIR-DRY 1"-THICK GREEN LUMBER TO 20 PERCENT MOISTURE CONTENT
Alder, Red	20–180
Ash, Black	60–200
Ash, Green	60–200
Ash, White	60–200
Aspen, Bigtooth	50–150
Aspen, Quaking	50–150
Basswood, American	40–150
Beech, American	70–200
Birch, Paper	40–200
Birch, Sweet	70–200
Birch, Yellow	70–200
Butternut	60–200
Cherry, Black	70–200
Cottonwood, Black	60–150
Cottonwood, Eastern	50–150
Elm, American	50–150
Elm, Rock	80–180
Hackberry	30–150
Hickory	60–200
Magnolia, Southern	40–150
Maple, Bigleaf	60–180
Maple, Red	30–120
Maple, Silver	30–120
Maple, Sugar	50–200
Oak, Northern Red	70–200
Oak, Northern White	80–250
Oak, Southern Red	100–300
Oak, Southern White (Chestnut)	120–320
Pecan	60–200
Sweet Gum, heartwood	70–300
Sweet Gum, sapwood	60–200
Sycamore, American	30–150
Tan Oak	180–365
Tupelo, Black	70–200
Tupelo, Water	70–200
Walnut, Black	70–200
Willow, Black	30–150
Yellow Poplar	40–150

DRYING TIME—SOFTWOODS

SPECIES	DAYS REQUIRED TO AIR-DRY 1"-THICK GREEN LUMBER TO 20 PERCENT MOISTURE CONTENT
Bald Cypress	100–300
Douglas Fir, Coast	20–200
Douglas Fir, Interior North	20–180
Douglas Fir, Interior South	10–100
Douglas Fir, Interior West	20–120
Hemlock, Eastern	90–200
Hemlock, Western	60–200
Larch, Western	60–120
Pine, Eastern White	60–200
Pine, Jack	40–200
Pine, Loblolly	30–150
Pine, Lodgepole	15–150
Pine, Longleaf	30–150
Pine, Ponderosa	15–150
Pine, Red	40–200
Pine, Shortleaf	30–150
Pine, Slash	30–150
Pine, Sugar (Light)	15–90
Pine, Sugar (Sinker)	45–200
Pine, Western White	15–150
Redwood, Light	60–185
Redwood, Sinker	200–365
Spruce, Engelmann	20–120
Spruce, Red	30–120
Spruce, Sitka	40–150
Spruce, White	30–120

WORKING PROPERTIES OF SOME HARDWOODS

All the information in this chart is based on actual tests. Use it to determine the likelihood of success when planing, shaping, turning, boring or sanding any of the hardwoods listed. For example, the chart shows that beech turns well (90 percent fair to excellent pieces), but it doesn't do so well when shaped (24 percent good to excellent pieces).

HARDWOOD	PLANING (1)	SHAPING (2)	TURNING (3)	BORING (4)	SANDING (5)
Alder, Red	61	20	88	64	*
Ash	75	55	79	94	75
Aspen	26	7	65	78	*
Basswood	64	10	68	76	17
Beech	83	24	90	99	49
Birch	63	57	80	97	34
Birch, Paper	47	22	*	*	*
Cherry, Black	80	80	88	100	*
Chestnut	74	28	87	91	64
Cottonwood	21	3	70	70	19
Elm, Soft	33	13	65	94	66
Hackberry	74	10	77	99	*
Hickory	76	20	84	100	80
Magnolia	65	27	79	71	37
Maple, Bigleaf	52	56	80	100	*
Maple, Hard	54	72	82	99	38
Maple, Soft	41	25	76	80	37
Oak, Red	91	28	84	99	81
Oak, White	87	35	85	95	83
Pecan	88	40	89	100	*
Sweet Gum	51	28	86	92	23
Sycamore	22	12	85	98	21
Tan Oak	80	39	81	100	*
Tupelo, Water	55	52	79	62	34
Tupelo, Black	48	32	75	82	21
Walnut, Black	62	34	91	100	*
Willow	52	5	58	71	24
Yellow Poplar	70	13	81	87	19

(1) percentage of perfect pieces
(2) percentage of good to excellent pieces
(3) percentage of fair to excellent pieces
(4) percentage of good to excellent pieces
(5) percentage of good to excellent pieces
*Test data not available.

APPROXIMATE RELATIVE HEARTWOOD DECAY RESISTANCE

The heartwood of a tree is the older portion of wood that extends from the tree center (also called the pith) to the sapwood. Unlike sapwood, the heartwood doesn't conduct sap and it no longer has living cells. Heartwood is usually darker and has better decay resistance than sapwood.

Decay resistance is important when choosing a wood that's to be used outdoors or in a damp environment. This list enables you to quickly compare the relative heartwood decay resistances of some common domestic woods.

Resistant or Very Resistant
Bald Cypress (old growth)
Catalpa
Cedars
Cherry, Black
Chestnut
Cypress, Arizona
Junipers
Locust, Black*
Mesquite
Mulberry, Red*
Oak, Bur
Oak, Chestnut
Oak, Gambel
Oak, Oregon White
Oak, Post
Oak, White
Osage Orange*
Redwood
Sassafras
Walnut, Black
Yew, Pacific*

Moderately Resistant
Bald Cypress (young growth)
Douglas Fir
Honey Locust
Larch, Western
Oak, Swamp Chestnut
Pine, Eastern White
Pine, Longleaf
Pine, Slash
• Tamarack

Slightly or Nonresistant
Alder
Ashes
Aspens
Basswood
Beech
Birches
Buckeye
Butternut
Cottonwood
Elms
Hackberry
Hemlocks
Hickories
Magnolia
Maples
Oak, Red
Oak, Black
Pines (except Eastern White, Longleaf and Slash)
Poplars
Spruces
Sweet Gums
True Firs
• Balsam Fir
• California Red Fir
• Fraser Fir
• Grand Fir
• Noble Fir
• Pacific Fir
• Subalpine Fir
• Willows
• Yellow Poplar

*Wood has exceptionally high decay resistance.

STEAM BENDING TABLE

Air-dried wood becomes quite pliable when heated to approximately 212° Fahrenheit. Bent wood has many woodworking applications including chair parts, curved railings and walking sticks.

This table shows the limiting steam-bending radius for several domestic and imported woods. The table is based on using good quality (straight-grained and free from defects) 1″-thick air-dried wood with a moisture content of 25 to 30 percent. The bending radius shown anticipates that up to 5 percent of the pieces could break during the bending process. Note that the use of a strap, which supports the stretched wood fibers during the bend, allows for a tighter radius.

The table is adapted from *The Wood Bending Handbook* by W.C. Stevens and N. Turner—an excellent book on the subject of bending wood. It's available from Woodcraft Supply, P.O. Box 1686, Parkersburg, WV 26102-1686.

COMMON NAME	BOTANICAL NAME	RADIUS (inches)	
		unsupported	supported with strap
Afrormosia	Pericopsis elata	29.0	14.0
Ash, American	Fraxinus spp.	13.0	4.5
Birch, Yellow*	Betula alleghaniensis	17.0	3.0
Crabwood	Carapa guianensis	48.0	30.0
Douglas Fir	Pseudotsuga menziesii	33.0	18.0
Ebony, African	Diospyros crassiflora	15.0	10.0
Elm, Rock	Ulmus thomasii	14.0	1.5
Elm, American	Ulmus americana	13.5	1.7
Hickory	Carya spp.	15.0	1.8
Iroko	Chlorophora excelsa	18.0	15.0
Jarrah*	Eucalyptus marginata	39.0	17.5
Mahogany, African	Khaya anthotheca	24.0	20.0
Mahogany, Honduras	Swietenia macrophylla	28.0	12.0
Oak, American White	Quercus spp.	13.0	.5
Oak, Red	Quercus rubra	11.5	1.0
Purpleheart	Peltogyne spp.	30.0	18.0
Ramin	Gonystylus bancanus	37.0	36.0
Teak	Tectona grandis	35.0	18.0

*Data from results of small-scale tests only.

CHAPTER 4

MANUFACTURED WOODS

SOFTWOOD PLYWOOD

Softwood plywood is used primarily for general construction applications such as wall and roof sheathing, siding and subflooring. In the woodworking shop, softwood plywood is used for jigs, fixture, shelves, shop cabinets and much more. When building furniture, however, softwood plywood is rarely used as a substrate for plastic laminate or high-quality veneer because the uneven plywood surfaces tend to be visible even after a veneer or laminate is applied.

Plywood is made by gluing thin sheets of wood, called veneers or plies, at right angles to each other. This cross-grain construction results in a wood product that is exceptionally strong. Also, it creates outstanding dimensional stability, which means the plywood changes little in length and width, even as the relative humidity changes.

Softwood plywood is almost always made using an odd number of veneers, usually three, five or seven. Using an odd number of veneers allows the grain of the two outside veneers (one in front and one in back) to run in the same direction.

During manufacture, small defects in the veneers (such as knots and splits) are removed with special cutters. A wood or synthetic plug (sometimes called a patch) is used to repair the cutout.

The American Plywood Association (APA) is the major trade association for the softwood plywood industry. Its member mills produce approximately 80 percent of the softwood plywood made in the United States. Most softwood plywood is made into $4' \times 8'$ panels, although $4' \times 9'$ and $4' \times 10'$ panels are also available.

STANDARD THICKNESSES

FRACTION (inches)	METRIC EQUIVALENT (millimeters)
$\frac{1}{4}$	6.4
$\frac{5}{16}$	7.9
$\frac{11}{32}$	8.7
$\frac{3}{8}$	9.5
$\frac{7}{16}$	11.1
$\frac{15}{32}$	11.9
$\frac{1}{2}$	12.7
$\frac{19}{32}$	15.1
$\frac{5}{8}$	15.9
$\frac{23}{32}$	18.3
$\frac{3}{4}$	19.1
$\frac{7}{8}$	22.2
1	25.4
$1\frac{3}{32}$	27.8
$1\frac{1}{8}$	28.6

SPECIES GROUP NUMBER

Softwood plywood is made from over seventy species of wood. The species are divided into five groups numbered in descending order of strength and stiffness, with Group 1 the highest and Group 5 the lowest.

GROUP 1	GROUP 2	GROUP 3	GROUP 4	GROUP 5
Apitong	Cedar, Port	Alder, Red	Aspen, Bigtooth	Basswood
Beech,	Orford	Birch, Paper	Aspen, Quaking	Poplar, Balsam
American	Cypress	Cedar, Alaska	Cativo	
Birch, Sweet	Douglas Fir 2*	Fir, Subalpine	Cedar, Incense	
Birch, Yellow	Fir, Balsam	Hemlock,	Cedar, Western	
Douglas Fir 1*	Fir, California	Eastern	Red	
Kapur	Red	Maple, Bigleaf	Cottonwood,	
Keruing	Fir, Grand	Pine, Jack	Eastern	
Larch, Western	Fir, Noble	Pine, Lodgepole	Cottonwood,	
Maple, Sugar	Fir, Pacific	Pine, Ponderosa	Black	
Pine, Caribbean	Silver	Pine, Spruce	(Western	
Pine, Loblolly	Fir, White	Redwood	Poplar)	
Pine, Longleaf	Hemlock,	Spruce,	Pine, Eastern	
Pine, Ocote	Western	Engelmann	White	
Pine, Shortleaf	Lauan, Almon	Spruce, White	Pine, Sugar	
Pine, Slash	Lauan, Bagtikan			
Tan Oak	Lauan, Mayapis			
	Lauan, Red			
	Lauan, Tangile			
	Lauan, White			
	Maple, Black			
	Mengkulang			
	Meranti, Red			
	Mersawa			
	Pine, Pond			
	Pine, Red			
	Pine, Virginia			
	Pine, Western			
	White			
	Spruce, Black			
	Spruce, Red			
	Spruce, Sitka			
	Sweet Gum			
	Tamarack			
	Yellow Poplar			

*Douglas Fir grown in Washington, Oregon, California, Idaho, Montana, Wyoming, Alberta and British Columbia are classified as Douglas Fir 1. Those grown in Nevada, Utah, Colorado, Arizona and New Mexico are classified as Douglas Fir 2.

EXPOSURE DURABILITY

Exposure durability classification is a measure of the strength of the softwood plywood glue bond as it relates to weather and the resulting moisture.

EXPOSURE DURABILITY CLASSIFICATION	DESCRIPTION
Exterior	Has a fully waterproof bond. Designed for permanent exposure to weather or moisture.
Exposure 1	Has a fully waterproof bond. Designed for applications where high moisture tions might be encountered in service, or where long construction delays are pected prior to providing protection.
Exposure 2	Intended for protected applications that could get occasional exposure to high ity and water leakage.
Interior	Made with interior glue; intended for interior applications only.

SOFTWOOD PLYWOOD OUTER VENEER GRADES

Softwood plywood outer veneers (face and back) are graded on the basis of natural growth characteristics of the wood and also the allowable size and number of repairs that may be made during manufacture. In addition to the grades below, some manufacturers also produce an "N" grade, which has the highest quality veneer and is available on special order only.

OUTER VENEER GRADE	DESCRIPTION
A	Has a smooth, paintable surface. Not more than 18 neatly made repairs perm Repairs can be wood or synthetic.
B	Has a solid surface. Shims, sled or router-type repairs and tight knots to 1" a grain permitted. Wood or synthetic repairs permitted. Some minor splits per
C Plugged	Improved C veneer. Splits limited to ⅛" width; knotholes or other open defects to ¼"×½". Wood or synthetic repairs permitted. Admits some broken grain.
C	Tight knots to 1½". Knotholes to 1" across grain and some to ½" if total wid knots and knotholes is within specified limits. Synthetic or wood repairs. Dis ation and sanding defects that do not impair strength are permitted. Limited allowed. Stitching permitted.
D	Knots and knotholes to 2½" width across grain and ½" larger within specifie Limited splits are permitted. Stitching permitted. Exposure durability classific limited to Exposure 1 or Interior.

GRADE DESIGNATIONS

Softwood plywood grades are usually identified in one of two ways, either (1) in terms of the veneer grade used on the face and back of the plywood or (2) by a name suggesting the plywood's intended use (including APA Performance Rated Panels).

Grade Designation by Face and Back Veneer Grades

A softwood plywood that's identified by the veneer grade on the face and back might be stamped A-B. Such a designation indicates that the face has an "A" grade veneer, while the back has a "B" grade veneer (see page 106, Softwood Plywood Outer Veneer Grades). Some other examples of grade combinations include A-A, B-C, B-D, and C-D.

Grade Designation by Intended Use

Plywood that is identified by a name suggesting the intended use might be stamped Underlayment or Marine. This grade designation also includes the APA Performance Rated Panels which are identified by such names as APA Rated Sheathing, APA Rated Sturd-I-Floor or APA Rated Siding.

SPAN RATINGS

APA Performance Rated Panels (APA Rated Sheathing, APA Rated Sturd-I-Floor and APA Rated Sidings) are further identified with a span rating. On APA Rated Sheathing, the span numbers are shown as two numbers separated by a slash, for example, 32/16 or 48/24. The left-hand number indicates the maximum recommended spacing of supports when the plywood is used for roof sheathing. The right-hand number indicates the maximum recommended spacing of supports when the plywood is used for subflooring. The span rating is shown as a single number on APA Rated Sturd-I-Floor and APA Rated Siding. All span ratings are based on installing the plywood panels with the long dimension across three or more supports.

GRADE MARK

Manufacturers label plywood with a *grade mark*. The grade mark provides useful information about the plywood product. Depending on the grade designation, the grade mark can be applied to the back or edge of the plywood.

Grade Mark for Plywood Identified by Face and Back Veneer Grades

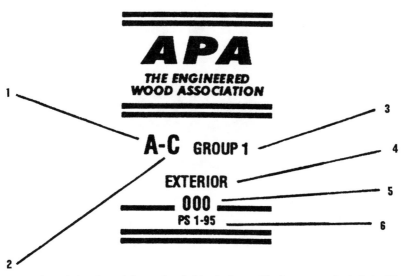

The grade mark for plywood that is identified by the face and back veneer grades includes (1) the grade of the face veneer, (2) the grade of the back veneer, (3) the species group number, (4) the exposure durability classification, (5) the lumber mill that produced the panel (shown as a number), and (6) the applicable product standard.

Grade Mark for Plywood Identified by Intended Use*

This grade mark can vary a bit, but in general includes (1) the panel grade designation, (2) the span rating, (3) the thickness, (4) the exposure durability classification, (5) the lumber mill that produced the panel (shown as a number), and (6) the applicable product standard.

*Grade mark shown is for an APA Performance Rated Panel.

HARDWOOD PLYWOOD

Hardwood plywood is used primarily for appearance applications. It provides an attractive wood surface that, as a general rule, costs less than solid-stock hardwood lumber of the same species. Also, because of its construction, hardwood plywood is dimensionally stable, which means that little expansion and contraction occurs as the relative humidity changes.

The plywood panel side that has the higher-grade outer veneer is called the face or the face side. The side with the lower-grade veneer is called the back. When the two outer veneers are the same grade, the panel doesn't have a back but rather has two face sides.

The material sandwiched between the two outer veneers is called the core. Hardwood plywood cores can be made from either softwood or hardwood veneer (not necessarily the same grade as the outer veneers), softwood or hardwood lumber, particleboard, medium-density fiberboard (MDF) or hardboard.

When hardwood plywood has five or more plies, the first layer of veneer under the outer veneer is called the crossband. The crossband is assembled at right angles (90°) to the grain of the outer veneer. In addition, the term crossbanding is used to describe all the inner layers of veneer that have a grain direction running at right angles to the outer veneers.

The type and quality of hardwood plywood can be affected by a variety of factors including (1) the wood species of the face veneer, (2) the grade of the face veneer, (3) the wood species of the back veneer, (4) the grade of the back veneer, (5) the construction of the core and (6) the type of glue bond.

When purchasing hardwood plywood, a number of thickness, width and length combinations are available. However, the most commonly found hardwood plywood panel sizes are 4′×6′, 4′×8′ and 4′×10′. Commonly found thicknesses are shown in the following chart. Other thicknesses might be available—check your dealer.

HARDWOOD PLYWOOD THICKNESSES

FRACTION (inches)	METRIC EQUIVALENT (millimeters)
⅛	3.2
¼	6.4
⅜	9.5
½	12.7
⅝	15.9
¾	19.1
⅞	22.2
1	25.4
1⅛	28.6

CATEGORIES OF WOOD SPECIES COMMONLY USED FOR FACE SIDES OF HARDWOOD PLYWOOD

Wood species most commonly used for the face side (or sides) of hardwood plywood are shown here. The species are grouped by category based primarily on the modulus of elasticity and specific gravity of the wood. The modulus of elasticity and specific gravity provide a measure of wood strength and stiffness. The categories are shown in descending order of strength and stiffness, with the highest values in category A and the lowest in category D.

You'll note that a few softwood species are shown in the chart. Softwoods that are considered decorative are used as face veneers on some hardwood plywoods.

Category A	Category B	Category C	Category D
Apitong	Ash, Black	Alder, Red	Aspen, Bigtooth
Ash, White	Avodire	Basswood	Aspen, Quaking
Beech, American	Birch, Paper	Butternut	Cedar, Eastern Red
Birch, Sweet	Cherry	Cativo	Cedar, Western
Birch, Yellow	Cucumber Tree	Chestnut	Red
Bubinga	Cypress	Cottonwood, Black	Willow, Black
Hickory	Elm, Rock	Cottonwood,	
Kapur	Fir, Douglas	Eastern	
• Dryobalanops	Fir, White	Elm, American	
spp.	Gum	Elm, Slippery	
Keruing	Hemlock, Western	Hackberry	
• Dipterocarpus	Magnolia,	Hemlock, Eastern	
spp.	Southern	Lauan	
Maple, Sugar	Mahogany, African	• Shorea spp.	
Oak, Red	Mahogany,	• Parashorea	
Oak, White	Honduras	spp.	
Pecan	Maple, Black	• Pentacme spp.	
Rosewood	Maple, Red	Maple, Silver	
Sapele	Spruce, Red	Merandi	
Tan oak	Spruce, Sitka	• Shorea spp.	
	Sycamore	Pine, Ponderosa	
	Teak	Pine, Sugar	
	Walnut, Black	Pine, Eastern	
	Yellow Poplar	White	
		Pine, Western	
		White	
		Primavera	
		Redwood	
		Sassafras	
		Spruce, Black	
		Spruce,	
		Engelmann	
		Spruce, White	
		Tupelo	

HARDWOOD PLYWOOD—STANDARD GRADES FOR FACE VENEERS

The grades, based primarily on appearance features, are shown in descending order of quality, with best appearance veneers in grade AA and the lowest in grade E.

GRADE	GENERAL DESCRIPTION
AA	Highest-quality veneer with an excellent appearance. For use in high-end applications such as quality furniture, case goods, doors and cabinets, and architectural paneling.
A	Allows a few more imperfections than grade AA but remains a high-quality panel.
B	Exhibits more imperfections than grade A, but still an attractive panel for many applications.
C, D and E	Veneer has sound surfaces, but allows unlimited color variation. Permits repairs that increase in size and number from grade C to grade E. Generally used where a more natural appearance is desired or where the surface is hidden.
SP (Specialty Grade)	Grade is limited to veneers that have characteristics unlike any found in grade AA through E. Species such as wormy chestnut and bird's-eye maple fall into grade SP. Acceptable characteristics are as agreed upon by buyer and seller.

HARDWOOD PLYWOOD—BACK GRADES

The grades are shown in descending order of quality, with grade 1 the highest and grade 4 the lowest.

IMPERFECTION	GRADE 1	GRADE 2	GRADE 3	GRADE 4
Sapwood	Yes	Yes	Yes	Yes
Discoloration and stain	Yes	Yes	Yes	Yes
Mineral streaks	Yes	Yes	Yes	Yes
Sound tight burls	Yes	Yes	Yes	Yes
Sound tight knots	Max. dia. ⅜″	Max. dia. ¾″	Max. dia. 1½″	Yes
Max. number of tight knots	16	16	Unlimited to ½″, max. 16 from ½″ to 1½″	Unlimited

IMPERFECTION	GRADE 1	GRADE 2	GRADE 3	GRADE 4
Knotholes	No	½″ repaired	1*	4
Max. combined number of knot-holes and re-paired knots	None**	All repaired; un-limited to ⅜″, no more than 8 from ⅜″ to ½″	Unlimited to ⅜″, no more than 10 from ⅜ to 1″*	Unlimited
Wormholes	Filled***	Filled***	Yes	Yes
Splits or open joints	Six ⅛″×12″ repaired	Six 3⁄16″×12″ repaired	Yes, ⅜″× ¼ length of panel*	1″ for ¼ panel length, ½ ″ for ½ panel length, ¼″ for full length of panel.
Doze (dote) and decay	Firm areas of doze	Firm areas of doze	Firm areas of doze	Areas of doze and decay OK provided ser-viceability not impaired.
Rough cut/rup-tured grain	Two 8″ diame-ter areas	5 percent of panel	Yes	Yes
Bark pockets	⅛″ wide repaired	¼″ wide repaired	Yes*	Yes
Laps	No	Repaired	Yes*	Yes

*Available repaired if necessary.
**Pin knots and repaired pin knots allowed.
***Unfilled wormholes shall be a maximum of 1⁄16″ dia.

INNER VENEER GRADES FOR VENEER-CORE HARDWOOD PLYWOOD

Grade designations are based on the allowable openings in the veneers.

DESCRIPTION	GRADE J	GRADE K	GRADE K	GRADE L	GRADE M
Thickness of crossbands adjacent to faces	Any thickness	Thicker than 1⁄10″	1⁄10″ and thinner	Any thickness	Any thickness
Knotholes and other simi-larly shaped openings (max. dia.)	None	⅜″	¾″	1″	2½″
Splits, gaps and other elongated end or edge openings. Each opening is visible on only one end or edge of panel (max. width).	⅛″	¼″	¼″	½″	1″

HARDWOOD PLYWOOD TYPES

Three hardwood plywood types are available. With each one the glue bond offers different moisture resistance qualities.

TYPE	DESCRIPTION
Technical (Exterior)	Fully waterproof. Meets panel construction criteria for special applications such as marine and aircraft.
Type I (Exterior)	Fully waterproof. Allows lower grade inner veneers than technical. Not to be used when continuously exposed to moisture in critical applications such as marine and aircraft.
Type II (Interior)	Moisture resistant, but not waterproof. For interior use only.

COMMON HARDWOOD PLYWOOD CORE CONSTRUCTIONS

Veneer-core: Made of veneers (usually three, five or seven) which can be either hardwood or softwood; species mixing not allowed.

Lumber-core: Made from three, five or seven plies of edge-glued solid lumber; can be either hardwood or softwood; species mixing not allowed. Grades available are Clear, Sound and Regular. A regular grade clear-edge version is available with edge strips at least 1½" wide to facilitate edge molding and shaping.

Banded lumber-core: Bands must be made from clear stock; other specifications are as agreed upon by buyer and seller. Bands can be applied to one or two ends (B1E, B2E); one or two sides (B1S, B2S); two ends, one side (B2E1S); two sides, one end (B2S1E); or two sides, two ends (B4).

Particleboard-core: Made with either three or five plies of particleboard.

MDF-core: Made with three plies of medium-density fiberboard.

Hardboard-core: Made with three plies of hardboard.

CHARACTERISTICS OF HARDWOOD PLYWOOD PANELS

CORE TYPE	FLATNESS	VISUAL EDGE QUALITY	SURFACE UNIFORMITY
Veneer Core (all hardwood)	Fair	Good	Good
Veneer Core (all softwood)	Fair	Good	Fair
Lumber Core (hardwood or softwood)	Good	Good	Good
Particleboard Core (medium density)	Excellent	Good	Excellent
MDF Core	Excellent	Excellent	Excellent
Hardboard Core (standard)	Excellent	Excellent	Excellent
Hardboard Core (tempered)	Excellent	Good	Good

DIMENSIONAL STABILITY	SCREW HOLDING	BENDING STRENGTH	AVAILABILITY
Excellent	Excellent	Excellent	Readily
Excellent	Excellent	Excellent	Readily
Good	Excellent	Excellent	Limited
Fair	Fair	Good	Readily
Fair	Good	Good	Readily
Fair	Good	Good	Readily
Good	Good	Good	Limited

MATCHING

Hardwood plywood face veneers can be matched in different ways to create panels that have considerable visual appeal. Face veneers are matched in one of three general ways:

1. Matching between adjacent veneers. Examples of matching between veneers include: book matching, slip matching, pleasing match, and random.
2. Matching of panel faces. Veneer is matched from one panel to another, usually to create symmetry in a room. Examples: running match, balance match and center match.
3. Matching for special effects. Examples: checkerboard match, diamond match and sunburst match.

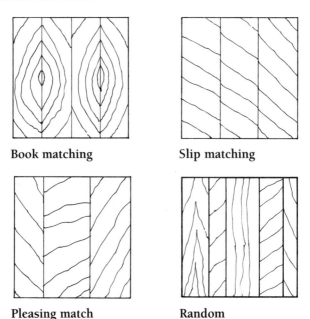

Book matching   Slip matching

Pleasing match   Random

TYPICAL HARDWOOD PLYWOOD EDGE STAMP

Hardwood plywood is labeled with a mill stamp that provides useful information about the panel. To avoid marring the face and back veneers, manufacturers generally stamp the panel edges with a mark called an edge stamp.

A typical edge stamp includes (1) the thickness of the plywood, (2) the grade of the face veneer, (3) the grade of the back veneer, (4) the wood species of the face, (5) the number of plies and type of core, (6) the identifying mill number and (7) the applicable standard.

1   2 3   4   5   6   7

1/2   A-1   BIRCH   7-PLY   MILL # [HPVA HP-1 199?

PARTICLEBOARD

Particleboard is made by mixing small particles of wood with synthetic resin and bonding them under heat and pressure. By modifying the manufacturing process, particleboard can be made into several different grades for various applications.

Particleboard grades are identified by a letter (or letters) followed by a hyphen and a number or letter. The letter designates the particleboard density as follows:

H = high density, generally above 50 pounds per cubic foot (pcf)
M = medium density, generally between 40 and 50 pcf
LD = low density, generally less than 40 pcf

The number following the hyphen indicates the grade identification within a particular density. For example, M-1 indicates medium density particleboard, grade 1. The higher the grade identification number, the higher the strength qualities of the particleboard. For example, grade M-2 has better strength characteristics than grade M-1.

Any special characteristics are listed after the grade identification number. For example, M-2-Exterior Glue indicates medium density particleboard, grade 2 made with exterior glue.

The chart below lists some of the important physical properties for each grade.

PARTICLEBOARD GRADES
(SELECTED REQUIREMENTS)

GRADE	MODULUS OF RUPTURE (psi)	MODULUS OF ELASTICITY (psi)	HARDNESS (pounds)	SCREW HOLDING	
				Face (pounds)	Edge (pounds)
H-1	2393	348,100	500	405	298
H-2	2973	348,100	1000	427	348
H-3	3408	398,900	1500	450	348
M-1	1595	250,200	500	NS[3]	NS[3]
M-S[2]	1813	275,600	500	202	180
M-2	2103	326,300	500	225	202
M-3	2393	398,900	500	247	225
LD-1	435	79,800	NS[3]	90	NS[3]
LD-2	725	148,700	NS[3]	124	NS[3]

Notes:
[1]Grades PBU, D-2 and D-3, used as flooring products, are not shown.
[2]Grade M-S refers to medium density "special" grade. This grade was added after grades M-1, M-2 and M-3 were established. Grade M-S falls between grades M-1 and M-2 in terms of physical properties.
[3]NS = not specified.

MEDIUM DENSITY FIBERBOARD (MDF)

Medium density fiberboard is made by mixing processed wood fibers with synthetic resin (or other suitable bonding system) and bonding them under heat and pressure. By modifying the manufacturing process, MDF can be made into several different grades for various applications. Thicknesses from ³⁄₁₆″ to 1½″ are available, but the ¾″ thickness is the one most commonly found.

MDF is organized into product classifications rather than grades. The classifications are based on the density of the product. A two-letter designation identifies each classification. The classifications are as follows:

HD = high density, generally above 50 pounds per cubic foot (pcf)
MD = medium density, generally between 40 and 50 pcf
LD = low density, generally less than 40 pcf

MDF products with special characteristics are identified with either a letter, a number or a term that identifies the characteristic. For example, MD-Exterior Glue indicates that the MDF has a medium density classification that meets exterior glue requirements.

The chart below lists some of the important physical properties for each grade.

MEDIUM DENSITY FIBERBOARD CLASSIFICATIONS
(SOME SELECTED REQUIREMENTS)

PRODUCT CLASSIFICATION	MODULUS OF RUPTURE (psi)	MODULUS OF ELASTICITY (psi)	SCREW HOLDING	
			Face (pounds)	Edge (pounds)
Interior MDF				
HD	5000	500,000	350	300
MD (.825″ thick or less)	3500	350,000	325	250
MD (more than .825″ thick)	3500	350,000	300	225
LD	2000	200,000	175	150
Exterior MDF				
MD-Exterior Glue (.825″ thick or less)	5000	500,000	325	250
MD-Exterior Glue (more than .825″ thick)	4500	450,000	300	225

HARDBOARD

Hardboard is made from wood chips that are converted into fibers and then bonded under heat and pressure. Other materials can be added to improve such characteristics as moisture and abrasion resistance, strength, stiffness and hardness. Hardboard is available either smooth-one-side (S1S) or smooth-both-sides (S2S).

HARDBOARD PANEL THICKNESSES

NOMINAL THICKNESS		THICKNESS RANGE (minimum–maximum)	
Inches	Millimeters	Inches	Millimeters
1/12 (.083)	2.1	.070–.090	1.8–2.3
1/10 (.100)	2.5	.091–.110	2.3–2.8
1/8 (.125)	3.2	.115–.155	2.9–3.9
3/16 (.188)	4.8	.165–.205	4.2–5.2
1/4 (.250)	6.4	.210–.265	5.3–6.7
5/16 (.312)	7.9	.290–.335	7.4–8.5
3/8 (.375)	9.5	.350–.400	8.9–10.2
7/16 (.438)	11.1	.410–.460	10.4–11.7
1/2 (.500)	12.7	.475–.525	12.1–13.3
5/8 (.625)	15.9	.600–.650	15.2–16.5
11/16 (.688)	17.5	.660–.710	16.8–18.0
3/4 (.750)	19.1	.725–.775	18.4–19.7
13/16 (.812)	20.6	.785–.835	19.9–21.2
7/8 (.875)	22.2	.850–.900	21.6–22.9
1 (1.000)	25.4	.975–1.025	24.8–26.0
1 1/8 (1.125)	28.6	1.115–1.155	28.3–29.4

HARDBOARD CLASSIFICATIONS

CLASS	GENERAL DESCRIPTION
Tempered	Highest strength, stiffness, hardness and resistance to water and abrasion. Available in all thicknesses from 1/12″ to 3/8″.
Standard	High strength and water resistance. Hardness and resistance to water and abrasion less than that of tempered class. Available in all thicknesses from 1/12″ to 3/8″.
Service-tempered	Has better strength, stiffness, hardness and resistance to water and abrasion than service class. Available in 1/8″, 3/16″, 1/4″ and 3/8″ thicknesses.
Service	Good strength, but not as strong as standard class. Available in 1/8″, 3/16″, 1/4″, 3/8″, 7/16″, 1/2″, 5/8″, 11/16″, 3/4″, 13/16″, 7/8″, 1″ and 1 1/8″ thicknesses.
Industrialite	Moderate strength. Available in 1/4″, 3/8″, 7/16″, 1/2″, 5/8″, 11/16″, 3/4″, 13/16″, 7/8″, 1″ and 1 1/8″ thicknesses.

CHAPTER 5

ADHESIVES

WOOD BONDING

When it comes to gluing ease, all woods are not created equal. As shown below, some woods are easier to glue than others. Highly dense or oily woods can be especially troublesome.

Woods That Bond Easily
Domestic Hardwoods:
  Alder
  Aspen
  Basswood
  Cottonwood
  Chestnut, American
  Magnolia
  Willow, Black
Domestic Softwoods:
  Cedar, Western Red
  Fir, Grand
  Fir, Noble
  Fir, Pacific
  Fir, White
  Pine, Eastern White
  Pine, Western White
  Redwood
  Spruce, Sitka
Imported Woods:
  Balsa
  Cativo
  Courbaril
  Hura
  Purpleheart
  Redwood
  Roble
  Spruce, Sitka

Woods That Bond Well
Domestic Hardwoods:
  Butternut
  Elm, American
  Elm, Rock
  Hackberry
  Maple, Soft
  Sweet Gum
  Sycamore
  Tupelo
  Walnut, Black
  Yellow Poplar

Domestic Softwoods:
  Cedar, Eastern Red
  Douglas Fir
  Larch, Western
  Pine, Sugar
  Pine, Ponderosa
Imported Woods:
  Afrormosia
  Andiroba
  Angelique
  Avodire
  Banak
  Iroko
  Jarrah
  Limba
  Mahogany, African
  Mahogany, South
    American
  Obeche
  Okoume
  Opepe
  Peroba Rosa
  Sapele
  Spanish Cedar
  Sucupira
  Wallaba

Woods That Bond Satisfactorily
Domestic Hardwoods:
  Ash, White
  Beech, American
  Birch, Sweet
  Birch, Yellow
  Cherry
  Hickory, Pecan
  Hickory, True
  Madrone
  Maple, Hard
  Oak, Red
  Oak, White

Domestic Softwoods:
  Cedar, Alaska
  Cedar, Port Orford
  Pine, Loblolly
  Pine, Longleaf
  Pine, Shortleaf
  Pine, Slash
Imported Woods:
  Angelin
  Azobe
  Benge
  Bubinga
  Karri
  Pau Marfim
  Parana Pine
  Pine, Caribbean
  Pine, Radiata
  Ramin

Woods That Bond With Difficulty
Domestic Hardwoods:
  Osage Orange
  Persimmon
Imported Woods:
  Balata
  Balau
  Greenheart
  Kaneelhart
  Kapur
  Keruing
  Lapacho
  Lignum Vitae
  Rosewood
  Teak

COMMONLY USED WOOD ADHESIVES

Adhesive properties can vary from one manufacturer to another. Always read the manufacturer's directions before starting.

ADHESIVE	COMMON NAME	EXAMPLES OF BRAND NAMES
Aliphatic resin	Yellow glue	Elmer's Carpenter's Glue Titebond Wood Glue
Contact cement	Contact cement	Weldwood Contact Cement
Cyanoacrylate	Super glue	Elmer's Wonder Bond Krazy Glue
Epoxy	Epoxy glue	Devcon 2-Ton Epoxy Industrial Formulators G-1
Hide glue (dry)	Animal glue	Behlen Ground Hide Glue Moser's Pearl Hide Glue
Hide glue (liquid)	Animal glue	Franklin's Hide Glue
Polyurethane	Polyurethane	Titebond Polyurethane Glue
Polyvinyl acetate	White glue	Elmer's Glue-All
Resorcinol	Waterproof glue	Elmer's Waterproof Glue Weldwood Waterproof Glue
Urea formaldehyde	Plastic resin	Weldwood Plastic Resin

ADVANTAGES	DISADVANTAGES	COMMON USES
Easy to use; water resistant (but not waterproof); water cleanup; economical.	Not waterproof (don't use on outdoor furniture).	All-purpose wood glue for interior use; stronger bond than polyvinyl acetate glue.
Bonds parts immediately.	Can't readjust parts after contact.	Bonding wood veneer or plastic laminate to substrate.
Bonds parts quickly.	Limited to small parts.	Bonding small parts made from a variety of materials.
Good gap filler; waterproof; fast setting formulas available; can be used to bond glass or metal to wood.	Requires mixing.	Bonding small parts made from a variety of materials.
Extended working time; water cleanup; economical.	Must be mixed with water and heated; poor moisture resistance (don't use on outdoor furniture).	Time-consuming assembly work; stronger bond than liquid hide glue; interior use only.
Easy to use; extended working time; water cleanup; economical.	Poor moisture resistance (don't use on outdoor furniture).	Time-consuming assembly work; interior use only.
Fully waterproof; gap-filling.	Eye and skin irritant.	Multi-purpose, interior and exterior applications including wood to wood, ceramic, plastic, Corian, stone, metal.
Easy to use, economical.	Not waterproof (don't use on outdoor furniture).	All-purpose wood glue for interior use; aliphatic resin glue has stronger bond.
Fully waterproof; extended working time.	Requires mixing; dark color shows glue line on most woods; long clamping time.	Outdoor furniture, marine applications.
Good water resistance; economical.	Requires mixing; long clamping time.	Outdoor furniture, cutting boards.

PROPERTIES OF COMMON WOODWORKING ADHESIVES*

ADHESIVE	FORM	PREPARATION	MINIMUM WORKING TEMPERATURE (degrees F)
Aliphatic resin	Liquid	Ready-to-use	45
Contact cement	Liquid	Ready-to-use	70
Cyanoacrylate	Liquid	Ready-to-use	40
Epoxy	Two-part liquid	Mix resin and hardener	Varies
Hide glue (dry)	Powder/flakes	Mix with water, heat (in glue pot) to 140–150°F.	–
Hide glue (liquid)	Liquid	Ready-to-use	72
Polyurethane	Liquid	Ready-to-use	50
Polyvinyl acetate	Liquid	Ready-to-use	60
Resorcinol	Powder and liquid resin	Mix powder and liquid resin	70
Urea formaldehyde	Powder	Mix with water	70

*Adhesive properties can vary from one manufacturer to another. Always read the manufacturer's directions before starting.

WORKING TIME	CLAMPING TIME (at 70° F)	CURE TIME	SOLVENT
5 to 7 minutes	1 to 2 hours	24 hours	Warm water
Up to 1 hour	No clamps; parts bond on contact	–	Acetone
30 seconds	10 to 60 seconds; clamps usually not required	30 minutes to several hours depending on brand	Acetone
5 to 60 minutes depending upon epoxy formula	5 minutes to several hours depending upon epoxy formula	3 hours and longer depending upon epoxy formula	Lacquer thinner
30 minutes	2 to 3 hours	24 hours	Warm water
5 minutes	2 to 3 hours	24 hours	Warm water
30 minutes	2 hours	8 hours	Mineral spirits while wet. Must abrade or scrape off when dry.
3 to 5 minutes	1 to 2 hours	24 to 48 hours	Warm water and soap
20 minutes	16 hours	12 hours	Cool water before hardening
15 to 30 minutes	16 hours	24 hours	Warm water and soap before hardening

CHAPTER 6

TOOLS

DRILL BIT SPEEDS

When boring wood, the optimum drill bit speed depends upon the type of bit you are using and the wood density (hardwood or softwood). The charts that follow provide suggested speeds for boring both softwoods and hardwoods when using twist drills, brad-point bits or Forstner bits. The speeds are based on using bits made from high-speed steel.

Wood densities can vary, even to some extent within the same species, so the charts should serve only as a general guide. Use slower speeds for boring deep holes or if the wood starts to burn. For intermediate sizes, use the speed for the next larger bit size.

SUGGESTED TWIST DRILL SPEEDS

BIT DIAMETER (inches)	REVOLUTIONS PER MINUTE (RPM)	
	Hardwood	Softwood
$\frac{1}{16}$	3500	3500
$\frac{1}{8}$	3250	3250
$\frac{3}{16}$	3000	3000
$\frac{1}{4}$	1800	2750
$\frac{5}{16}$	1500	2500
$\frac{3}{8}$	1200	2250
$\frac{7}{16}$	900	1750
$\frac{1}{2}$	750	1500
$\frac{5}{8}$	600	1250
$\frac{3}{4}$	500	800

SUGGESTED BRAD-POINT BIT SPEEDS

BIT DIAMETER (inches)	REVOLUTIONS PER MINUTE (RPM)	
	Hardwood	Softwood
$\frac{1}{8}$	1000	1700
$\frac{3}{16}$	950	1650
$\frac{1}{4}$	900	1600
$\frac{5}{16}$	800	1550
$\frac{3}{8}$	750	1500
$\frac{7}{16}$	700	1450
$\frac{1}{2}$	600	1400
$\frac{5}{8}$	400	1300
$\frac{3}{4}$	350	1200
$\frac{7}{8}$	300	1100
1	250	1000

SUGGESTED FORSTNER BIT SPEEDS

BIT DIAMETER (inches)	REVOLUTIONS PER MINUTE (RPM)	
	Harwood	Softwood
¼	1000	2000
⁵⁄₁₆	975	1950
⅜	950	1900
⁷⁄₁₆	925	1850
½	900	1800
⅝	850	1700
¾	800	1600
⅞	750	1500
1	700	1400
1⅛	600	1200
1¼	500	1000
1½	350	700
1¾	300	600
2	250	500

SUGGESTED WOOD LATHE SPEEDS

The best lathe speed for a given wood turning task is dictated by the size of the stock and the type of cut to be made. As the stock size increases, the lathe speed is reduced. Also, roughing cuts require slower speeds than shaping cuts or sanding.

STOCK DIAMETER (inches)	ROUGHING CUT (rpm)	SHAPING CUT (rpm)	SANDING (rpm)
under 2	800 to 1200	2400 to 2800	3000 to 4000
2 to 4	600 to 1000	1800 to 2400	2400 to 3000
over 4 to 6	600 to 800	1200 to 1800	1800 to 2400
over 6 to 8	400 to 600	800 to 1200	1200 to 1800
over 8 to 10	300 to 400	600 to 800	900 to 1200
over 10 to 12	250 to 300	300 to 600	600 to 800

BAND SAW BLADE MINIMUM CUTTING RADIUS

The minimum cutting radius of a band saw blade is directly related to the width of the blade. As the blade width increases, so, too, does the minimum cutting radius. For maximum control and the smoothest cut, use the widest blade that can meet your minimum radius requirement.

BLADE WIDTH (inches)	MINIMUM CUTTING RADIUS (inches)
⅛	¼
³⁄₁₆	½
¼	¾
⅜	1¼
½	2½
¾	3

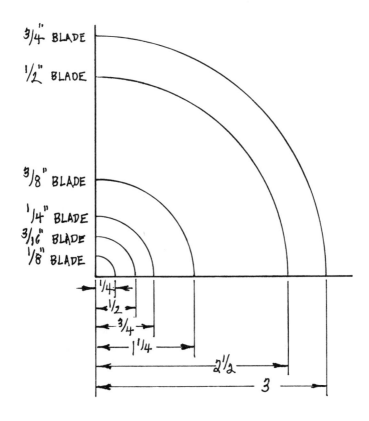

BAND SAW BLADE TOOTH STYLES

Band saw blades are available in three tooth styles: standard tooth (also called regular), hook tooth (also called saber tooth) and skip tooth. Each tooth style offers somewhat different cutting characteristics.

As shown in the illustrations, band saw blade teeth are cut at an angle called the rake angle. Teeth cut at a 90° angle to the back of the blade have a rake angle of 0°. Standard tooth and skip-tooth blades have 0° rake angles. Blades with a 0° rake angle tend to cut slower, but the cuts are relatively smooth. Hook tooth blades have a rake angle of 10°. Blades with a 10° rake angle can cut faster, but the cuts are going to be relatively rough.

The number of blade teeth per inch (tpi) is called the pitch. The pitch can vary from 2 to 24 depending upon the blade style and width. A blade with many teeth per inch has a "fine pitch," while one with few teeth per inch has a "coarse pitch." Keep in mind that, when making any cut, the blade must have at least three teeth into the material.

TOOTH TYPE	AVAILABLE WIDTHS (inches)	PITCH RANGE (tpi)	DESCRIPTION
Standard or Regular	1/16 to 1	6 to 24	0° rake, smooth cut but with increased heat. Teeth closely spaced. Good for thin, dense wood and for cutting across grain.
Hook or Saber	1/4 to 1	2 to 6	10° rake makes it an aggressive blade. Especially good for cutting thick stock parallel to the grain.
Skip	3/16 to 1	3 to 6	0° rake. A widely used blade. Cuts faster, especially parallel to grain, but cut is coarse. Good for resawing. Not as good as standard tooth or hook tooth for cutting across grain.

DETERMINING BAND SAW BLADE LENGTH

If you've lost the owner's manual for your band saw and can't remember the blade length, here's an easy formula for calculating the correct length.

$L = (2 \times A) + (3.14 \times B)$

where:

L = band saw blade length (in inches)

A = distance between the band saw wheel center lines (in inches)

B = diameter of either the upper or lower wheel (in inches)

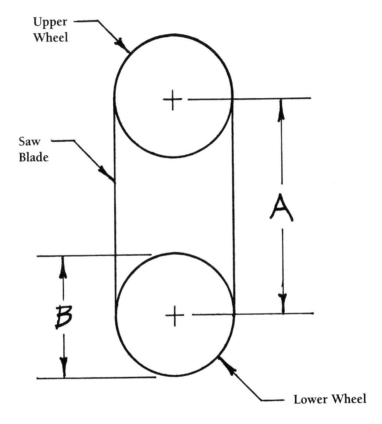

Upper Wheel

Saw Blade

A

B

Lower Wheel

Note: Before measuring the A dimension, locate the adjustable upper (tension) wheel so that it is midway between the fully up and fully down positions.

SCROLL SAW BLADES

Scroll saw blades are available in several popular tooth styles including standard tooth (also called skip tooth or fretsaw), scroll saw tooth and spiral tooth. Other tooth styles may also be available. The blade width, blade thickness and teeth per inch can vary slightly from one manufacturer to another.

Standard

Scroll

Spiral

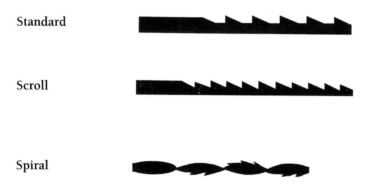

STANDARD TOOTH BLADES

UNIVERSAL NUMBER	BLADE WIDTH (inches)	BLADE THICKNESS (inches)	TEETH PER INCH	APPLICATION
2/0	.022	.010	28	For intricate cutting of wood,
0	.024	.011	25	plastic and hard rubber. Cuts
1	.026	.012	24	material from $\frac{1}{16}''$ to $\frac{1}{4}''$ thick.
2	.029	.012	20	For tight radius cutting of wood
3	.032	.013	18	and plastics. Cuts material from
4	.035	.015	15	$\frac{3}{32}''$ to $\frac{1}{2}''$ thick.
5	.038	.016	12½	For close radius cutting of wood
6	.041	.016	12½	and plastics. Cuts material $\frac{1}{8}''$ thick and heavier.
7	.045	.017	11½	For cutting wood and plastics.
8	.048	.018	11½	Cuts material from $\frac{3}{16}''$ to 2"
9	.053	.018	11½	thick.
10	.059	.019	11	
11	.059	.019	9½	
12	.062	.024	9½	

SCROLL SAW TOOTH BLADES

UNIVERSAL NUMBER	BLADE WIDTH (inches)	BLADE THICKNESS (inches)	TEETH PER INCH	APPLICATION
—	.049	.022	25	For tight radius cutting of hardwoods and softwoods. Makes smooth finish cuts in materials from 3/32″ to 1/4″ thick.
—	.070	.023	20	
—	.110	.022	20	For hardwoods and softwoods. Makes medium smooth finish cuts in materials from 3/32″ to 1/4″ thick.
—	.110	.022	10	For hardwoods, softwoods and plastics. Makes medium finish cuts in materials from 1/4″ to 3/4″ thick.
—	.187	.025	10	
—	.250	.028	7	

SPIRAL TOOTH BLADES

Spiral tooth blades have 360° cutting capacity so you don't have to turn the workpiece.

UNIVERSAL NUMBER	KERF THICKNESS (inches)	TEETH PER INCH
0	.032	46
2	.035	41
4	.041	36
5	.047	36

SABER SAW BLADES

Blades for the saber saw (also called the jigsaw) are available in a variety of styles for cutting a wide range of materials. Indeed, one manufacturer makes over a dozen different blade styles. Some of the commonly used wood cutting blades are shown here.

ALL-PURPOSE WOOD AND COMPOSITION BLADES

Application: Fine-tooth (10 tpi), medium-tooth (7 tpi) and coarse-tooth (5 tpi) cut wood up to ¾" thick. Blade length is 3".

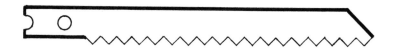

CARBIDE-COATED BLADES

Application: Medium grit cuts softwood plywood and hardwood veneer plywood. Blade length is 2⅞".

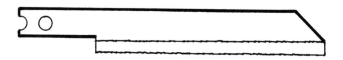

KNIFE-EDGE BLADE

Application: Veneer cutting. Blade length is 2½".

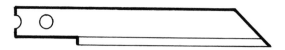

FLUSH BLADE

Application: Permits flush cuts in corners, other tight locations. Blade length is 3".

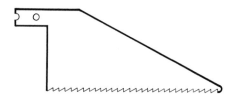

PULLEY FORMULAS

Table saws, band saws, jointers, drill presses and lathes often incorporate a pair of pulleys and a V-belt to transfer power from the motor to the business end of the machine. When two pulleys operate from a common V-belt, they relate to each other according to the following formula:

$$A \times B = C \times D$$

where:

A = speed (in rpm) of the motor
B = diameter (in inches) of the driver (motor) pulley
C = speed (in rpm) of the driven pulley
D = diameter (in inches) of the driven pulley

Note: The motor speed (in rpm) is usually stamped on the motor nameplate.

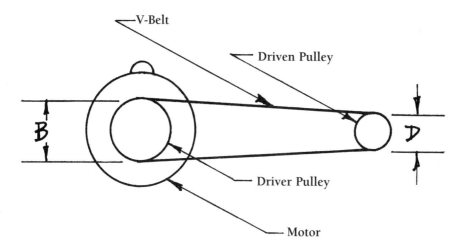

The above formula can be rewritten, producing four additional formulas as follows:

$$A = C \times D/B \qquad C = A \times B/D$$
$$B = C \times D/A \qquad D = A \times B/C$$

WORKSHOP APPLICATION

A lathe motor operates at 1725 rpm and has a 4″ diameter pulley. The motor pulley is connected by V-belt to a 2″ pulley that turns the headstock. What is the lathe speed?

The following are known:

A = 1725 rpm
B = 4″
C = driven pulley speed = lathe speed
D = 2″

Since C is unknown, use the formula:

$$C = A \times B/D$$
$$= 1725 \times 4/2$$
$$= 6900/2$$
$$= 3450 \text{ rpm}$$

COMMON ROUTER BIT PROFILES

Router bits are manufactured in dozens of different profiles for a wide variety of woodworking applications. The fourteen bits shown here represent profiles most commonly used by both hobbyist and professional woodworkers.

Bit sizes are also listed, although not all of the sizes are going to be found at your local hardware store. The angles are shown in degrees; all other dimensions are in inches.

Router bits are generally made from high-speed steel, solid carbide or carbide-tipped steel. Pilots are fixed or ball-bearing guided. Shanks can be ¼″ or ½″ diameter.

All dimensions are in inches unless otherwise noted.

Straight

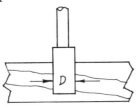

Diameter (D): ¹⁄₁₆, ³⁄₃₂, ⅛, ⁵⁄₃₂, ³⁄₁₆, ¼, ⁹⁄₃₂, ⁵⁄₁₆, ⅜, ⁷⁄₁₆, ½, ⁹⁄₁₆, ⅝, ¹¹⁄₁₆, ¾, ¹³⁄₁₆, ⅞, 1, 1⅛, 1¼, 1⅜, 1½, 1¾

Chamfer

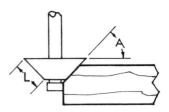

Cutting Angle (A): 15°, 22½°, 25°, 30°, 45°
Cutting Length (L): ½, ⅝, ¾, 1

Round Nose (Core Box)

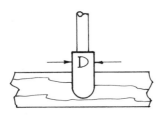

Diameter (D): ⅛, ³⁄₁₆, ¼, ⅜, ½, ⅝, ¾, 1, 1¼, 1½, 2

V-Groove

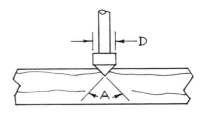

Diameter (D): ¼, ⅜, ½, ⅝, ¾, ⅞, 1, 1½, 2
Cutting Angle (A): 90° (60° angles available in a few sizes)

Cove

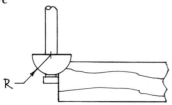

Radius (R): ¹⁄₁₆, ⅛, ³⁄₁₆, ¼, ⁵⁄₁₆, ⅜, ½, ⅝, ¾

Round Over

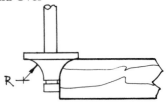

Radius (R): ¹⁄₁₆, ⅛, ⁵⁄₃₂, ³⁄₁₆, ¼, ⁵⁄₁₆, ⅜, ½, ⅝, ¾, ⅞, 1, 1⅛, 1¼, 1⅜, 1½

Beading

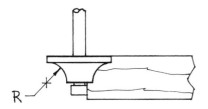

Radius (R): $\frac{1}{16}$, $\frac{1}{8}$, $\frac{5}{32}$, $\frac{3}{16}$, $\frac{1}{4}$, $\frac{5}{16}$, $\frac{3}{8}$, $\frac{1}{2}$, $\frac{5}{8}$, $\frac{3}{4}$, $\frac{7}{8}$, 1, $1\frac{1}{8}$, $1\frac{1}{4}$, $1\frac{3}{8}$, $1\frac{1}{2}$

Roman Ogee

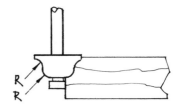

Radius (R): $\frac{5}{32}$, $\frac{1}{4}$

Classical Cove and Bead

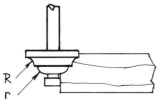

Large radius (R): $\frac{1}{4}$; small radius (r): $\frac{5}{32}$
Large radius (R): $\frac{5}{32}$; small radius (r): $\frac{5}{32}$
Large radius (R): $\frac{1}{4}$; small radius (r): $\frac{1}{4}$

Dovetail

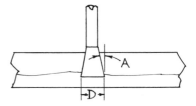

Diameter (D): $\frac{1}{4}$, $\frac{5}{16}$, $\frac{3}{8}$, $\frac{1}{2}$, $\frac{5}{8}$, $\frac{11}{16}$, $\frac{3}{4}$, $\frac{13}{16}$

Cutting angles (A): 7°, $7\frac{1}{2}$°, 8°, 9°, 10°, 14°, 18° (cutting angles are not available for all diameters shown)

Flush Trim

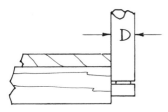

Diameter (D): $\frac{1}{4}$, $\frac{3}{8}$, $\frac{1}{2}$, $\frac{3}{4}$, $\frac{7}{8}$

Rabbeting

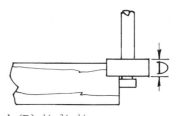

Depth (D): $\frac{1}{4}$, $\frac{3}{8}$, $\frac{1}{2}$

Half-Round

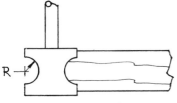

Radius (R): $\frac{3}{32}$, $\frac{1}{8}$, $\frac{3}{16}$, $\frac{1}{4}$, $\frac{3}{8}$, $\frac{1}{2}$, $\frac{5}{8}$

Vertical Raised Panel

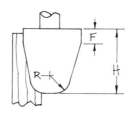

Radius (R): $\frac{3}{8}$; flat (F): $\frac{3}{8}$; height (H): $1\frac{5}{8}$

COMMON MOLDING HEAD CUTTER PROFILES

A table or radial arm saw equipped with a molding head can cut a wide variety of profiles and moldings. Shown here are some of the popular cutter profiles.

All dimensions are in inches.

Straight

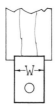

Width (W): 1

Cove

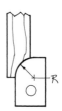

Radius (R): ⅝

Cove and Bead

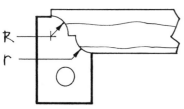

Large radius (R): ⁵⁄₁₆
Small radius (r): ⁵⁄₁₆

Quarter Round

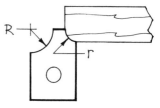

Large radius (R): ½
Small radius (r): ¼

V-Groove

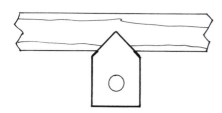

Clover-Leaf

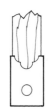

Flute

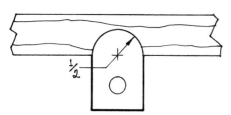

Radius: ½

Tongue

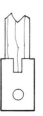

Groove

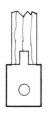

Three-Bead

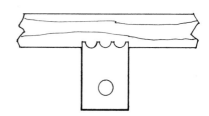

Glue Joint

Door Lip

Bead and Batten

Base Molding

TABLE AND RADIAL ARM SAW BLADES

Blades for table and radial arm saws fall into two broad categories: (1) those made entirely from steel and (2) those made from steel, but with teeth that are tipped with tungsten carbide.

An all-steel blade is typically made from either carbon steel or high-speed steel. Although it won't last as long as a carbide-tipped blade, an all-steel blade costs less, so it is probably the more economical choice if the blade is going to get only occasional use.

Carbide-tipped blades cost more than all-steel blades, but the carbide tips stay sharper for considerably longer. Indeed, a carbide-tipped blade can cut up to 50 times longer than an all-steel blade before sharpening is required. And carbide-tipped blades are even more effective when cutting particleboard, MDF and hardboard.

A number of blade designs are available, but those most commonly used are the crosscut blade, rip blade and combination blade. Other designs include specialty blades such as plywood cutting blades, laminate cutting blades, thin kerf blades and others.

BLADE	APPLICATION

Crosscut

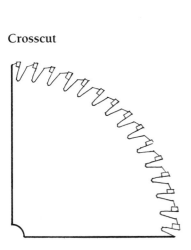

For cutting across the grain or at a diagonal. Has more teeth than rip or combination blades, resulting in a smoother cut with a minimum of splintering. Blade shown is carbide-tipped.

Rip

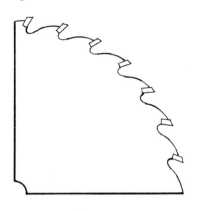

For cutting with (parallel to) the grain. Requires fewer and larger teeth than crosscut blades. Cut is relatively rough. Blade shown is carbide-tipped.

Combination

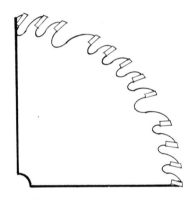

For both crosscutting and ripping. The number and size of the teeth are a compromise between the crosscut and rip blade designs. Eliminates having to constantly change from rip blade to crosscut blade. A good general purpose blade for all cuts, but it doesn't rip as well as a rip blade or crosscut as well as a crosscut blade. Blade shown is carbide-tipped.

Specialty Blades

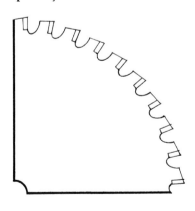

Plywood blade shown, but specialty blades also include laminate-cutting blades, thin kerf blades and others. Blade shown is carbide-tipped.

TABLE SAW COVING CUTS

The table saw can be used to make coving cuts that produce some interesting profiles. The workpiece, supported by an auxiliary fence clamped to the saw table, is slowly passed through the saw blade at an angle to create the cove. The first pass is made with the blade elevated no more than $\frac{1}{16}''$ above the saw table. After each subsequent pass, the blade is raised in $\frac{1}{16}''$ increments until the full cutting depth is reached.

The profile of the cove depends upon three factors: (1) the angle at which the stock is passed through the blade, (2) the diameter of the saw blade and (3) the height of the saw blade when the last cutting pass is made. On the next page are examples of $\frac{3}{4}''$ deep coves cut at angles of 45, 50, 55, 60, 65, 70 and 75° using a 10″ diameter saw blade.

For safety's sake, make sure the auxiliary fence is securely attached to the saw table. Also, be sure to use a push stick and keep hands well away from the blade. And always advance the workpiece slowly through the blade.

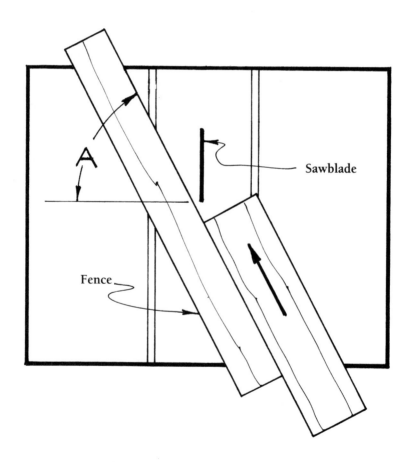

Sawblade

Fence

Angle A (see previous page) (in degrees)	Profile
45	
50	
55	
60	
65	
70	
75	

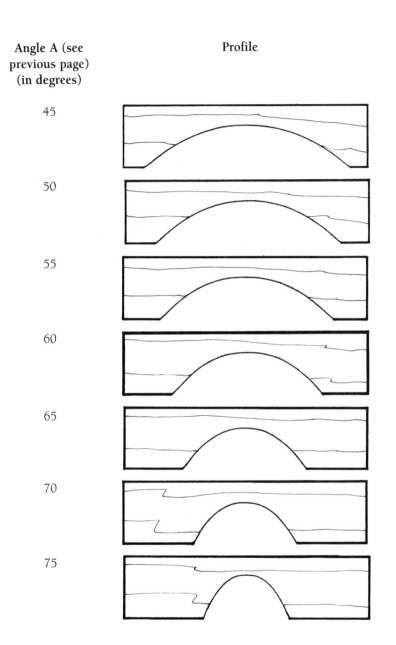

MANUFACTURERS' CUSTOMER SERVICE TELEPHONE NUMBERS

Accuride
Tel. (310) 903-0200

AEG
Tel. (800) 729-3878

Amana Tool Corp.
Tel. (800) 445-0077

AMT
Tel. (800) 435-3279

Black and Decker
Tel. (800) 762-6672

Bosch Power Tools
Tel. (800) 815-8665

Delta
Tel. (800) 223-7278

DeWalt
Tel. (800) 433-9258

Dremel
Tel. (800) 437-3635

Eagle America
Tel. (216) 286-7429

Freud USA, Inc.
Tel. (800) 472-7307

Klingspor Abrasives, Inc.
Tel. (800) 645-5555

Makita
Tel. (800) 462-5482

Metabo
Tel. (800) 638-2264

Milwaukee Electric Tool Co.
Tel. (800) 729-3878

Panasonic
Tel. (201) 392-6913

Porter-Cable
Tel. (800) 321-9443

Powermatic
Tel. (800) 248-0144

Ryobi America Corp.
Tel. (800) 525-2579

Sears Power and Hand Tools
Contact nearest Sears store.

Skil
Tel. (800) 815-8665

Titebond
Tel. (800) 472-7307

CHAPTER 7

SHARPENING

SHARPENING ANGLES

In order to cut effectively, each of the various cutting tools used for woodworking must be sharpened to a specific angle. The sharpening angles for the most commonly used wood tools are shown here.

CHISELS

Note: Sharpen to 30° if you do a lot of mortising or deep cutting.

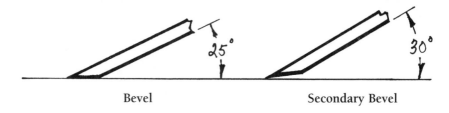

Bevel   Secondary Bevel

PLANE IRONS

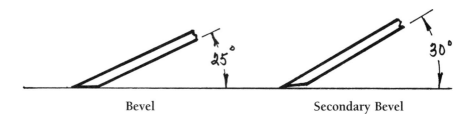

Bevel   Secondary Bevel

SPOKESHAVES

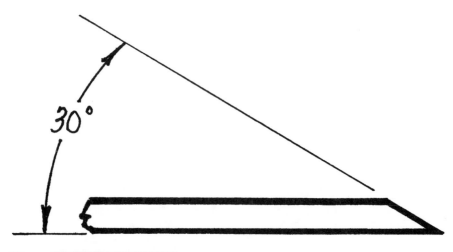

DRAWKNIVES

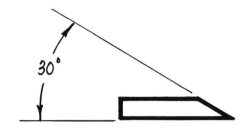

JOINTER BLADES

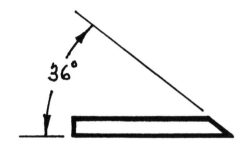

CARVING GOUGES

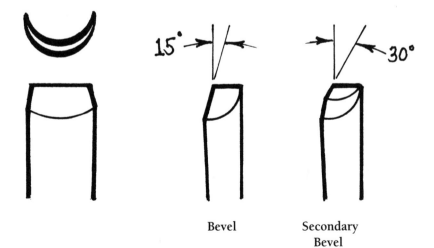

Bevel   Secondary
Bevel

TURNING CHISELS

Gouge

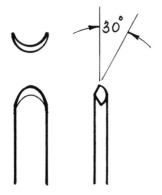

Skew

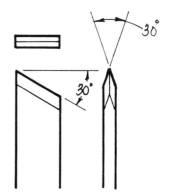

Parting Tool

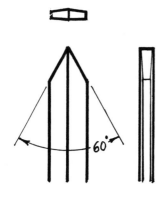

Spear Point

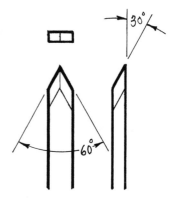

Flat Nose

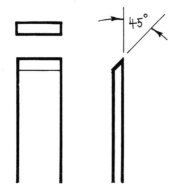

Round Nose

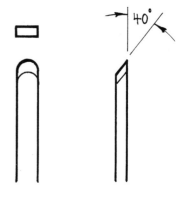

TYPES OF BENCH SHARPENING STONES

STONE TYPE	DESCRIPTION
Aluminum oxide (tradename: India)	Man-made oilstone. Available in coarse, medium and fine grits.
Silicon carbide (tradename: Crystolon)	Man-made oilstone. Available in coarse, medium and fine grits.
Soft Arkansas	Natural oilstone, medium grit.
Hard Arkansas	Natural oilstone, fine grit.
Hard black Arkansas	Natural oilstone, extra-fine grit.
Japanese water stones	Man-made water stone (natural stones are marketed but extremely expensive). Available in grits from 80 to 8000.
Diamond	Man-made stone. Available in extra-coarse, coarse, fine, and extra-fine.
Ceramic	Man-made stone. Available in medium, fine and ultra-fine grits.

COMPARISON OF U.S. AND JAPANESE GRITS

The United States and Japanese use different grit systems for sharpening stones. This chart lists U.S. grits and the approximate Japanese equivalents.

U.S. GRIT	JAPANESE GRIT
100	150
180	240
240	280
280	360
320	500
350	600
500	1000
700	2000
900	4000

Chart courtesy Woodcraft Supply Corporation.

SELECTING A BENCH SHARPENING STONE

SHARPENING APPLICATION	SUGGESTED STONE
Substantial metal removal for: • cleaning up a nicked edge or • changing a bevel angle or • reshaping a cutting edge	Coarse aluminum oxide, coarse silicon carbide, Japanese water stones under 300 grit or extra-coarse diamond.
Moderate metal removal for: • smoothing the rough surface created by the previous step or • smoothing an edge that's dull but not damaged	Medium aluminum oxide, medium silicon carbide, 1000-grit Japanese water stone or coarse diamond.
Light metal removal for: • smoothing the moderately-rough surface created by the previous step	Fine aluminum oxide, fine silicon carbide, 1200-grit Japanese water stones, soft Arkansas or fine diamond.
Very light metal removal (honing) for: • smoothing the light scratches from the previous step and • removing the wire burr on the back of the blade	Japanese water stones above 2000-grit, hard Arkansas fine ceramic, fine diamond.
Polishing	Japanese water stones above 6000-grit, hard black Arkansas, ultra-fine ceramic, extra-fine diamond.

CHAPTER 8

FASTENERS

WOOD SCREW HEAD OPTIONS

Wood screws are available in three head options: flathead, roundhead and ovalhead. In addition, flathead screws have three commonly available drive options: slotted, Phillips and square.

    Note that the length of a wood screw is measured from the end of the screw to the widest part of the screw head.

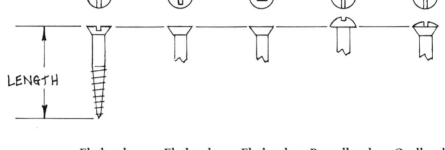

Flathead	Flathead	Flathead	Roundhead	Ovalhead
Slotted	Phillips	Square	Slotted	Slotted
Drive	Drive	Drive	Drive	Drive

WOOD SCREW SHANK DIAMETERS

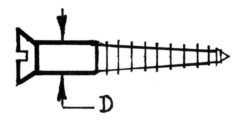

SCREW NUMBER	SHANK DIAMETER (D)	SCREW NUMBER	SHANK DIAMETER (D)
0	.060	9	.177
1	.073	10	.190
2	.086	12	.216
3	.099	14	.242
4	.112	16	.268
5	.125	18	.294
6	.138	20	.320
7	.151	24	.372
8	.164		

WOOD SCREW LENGTHS AND COMMONLY AVAILABLE SCREW NUMBERS

LENGTH (inches)	COMMONLY AVAILABLE SCREW NUMBERS
¼	0, 1, 2, 3
⅜	2, 3, 4, 5, 6, 7
½	2, 3, 4, 5, 6, 7, 8
⅝	3, 4, 5, 6, 7, 8, 9, 10
¾	4, 5, 6, 7, 8, 9, 10
⅞	6, 7, 8, 9, 10, 12
1	6, 7, 8, 9, 10, 12, 14
1¼	6, 7, 8, 9, 10, 12, 14, 16
1½	6, 7, 8, 9, 10, 12, 14, 16, 18
1¾	7, 8, 9, 10, 12, 14, 16, 18
2	8, 9, 10, 12, 14, 16, 18, 20
2¼	10, 12, 14, 16, 18, 20
2½	12, 14, 16, 18, 20
2¾	14, 16, 18, 20
3	16, 18, 20
3½	16, 18, 20
4	18, 20

DRYWALL (SHEETROCK) SCREWS

Designed for securing drywall to wooden studs, this screw has found favor with many woodworkers. Unlike a wood screw, which has a tapered body, a drywall screw has the same body diameter throughout its length. The result is a thread that is sharper and deeper. Drywall screws are generally available in sizes 4, 6, 7, 8, 9, 10 and 12 and in a variety of lengths.

The screws are hardened, making them tough, but they tend to be brittle. However, when used with some softwoods, the screws can often be driven without drilling shank or pilot holes.

Also available is a version that has a double-lead thread. It is designed to be used with steel studs but is not as effective with wood.

PARTICLEBOARD AND MEDIUM DENSITY FIBERBOARD (MDF) SCREWS

Like drywall screws, particleboard and MDF screws do not have tapered bodies.

They have deep, sharp threads that are able to hold effectively in both particleboard and MDF.

Particleboard and MDF screws have a flat head and a Phillips or square drive. The screws are available in a limited number of sizes and lengths.

CONVERTING PENNY SIZE TO NAIL LENGTH

The word "penny," represented by a lower-case "d," is used to specify the length of common, casing, finishing and several other types of nails.

PENNY SIZE	NAIL LENGTH (inches)	PENNY SIZE	NAIL LENGTH (inches)
2d	1	10d	3
3d	1¼	12d	3¼
4d	1½	16d	3½
5d	1¾	20d	4
6d	2	30d	4½
7d	2¼	40d	5
8d	2½	50d	5½
9d	2¾	60d	6

NAIL GAUGES AND EQUIVALENT DIAMETERS

PENNY SIZE	COMMON NAIL		CASING NAIL		FINISHING NAIL	
	Gauge	Diameter (inches)	Gauge	Diameter (inches)	Gauge	Diameter (inches)
2d	15	.072	15½	.067	16½	.058
3d	14	.080	14½	.073	15½	.067
4d	12½	.095	14	.080	15	.072
5d	12½	.095	14	.080	14	.080
6d	11½	.113	12½	.095	13½	.086
7d	11½	.113	12½	.095	13	.092
8d	10¼	.131	11½	.113	12½	.095
9d	10¼	.131	11½	.113	12½	.095
10d	9	.148	10½	.128	11½	.113
12d	9	.148	10½	.128	11½	.113
16d	8	.162	10	.135	11	.121
20d	6	.192	9	.148	10	.135
30d	5	.207	9	.148	—	—
40d	4	.225	8	.162	—	—
50d	3	.244	—	—	—	—
60d	2	.262	—	—	—	—

NAILS PER POUND

PENNY SIZE   NUMBER OF NAILS PER POUND (approximate)

	Common (uncoated)	Casing (uncoated)	Finishing (uncoated)
2d	875	1010	1350
3d	570	635	810
4d	315	475	585
5d	270	405	500
6d	180	235	310
7d	160	210	240
8d	105	145	190
9d	95	130	170
10d	70	95	120
12d	65	90	112
16d	50	70	90
20d	30	50	60
30d	24	46	—
40d	18	35	—
50d	16	—	—
60d	11	—	—

STANDARD MACHINE THREADS

The threads shown here, which are based on the Unified National Standard, are used on machine bolts, machine screws, threaded rod and other fasteners. Coarse threads (UNC) are suitable for most general applications. Fine threads (UNF) are sometimes used for the assembly of jigs, fixtures and machine components. Extra-fine threads (UNEF) are primarily used in the automotive and aircraft industries, although there can be occasional woodworking applications.

NOMINAL SIZE (inches)	MAJOR DIAMETER (inches)*	THREADS PER INCH		
		Coarse (UNC)	Fine (UNF)	Extra-Fine (UNEF)
1	.0730	64	72	—
2	.0860	56	64	—
3	.0990	48	56	—
4	.1120	40	48	—
5	.1250	40	44	—
6	.1380	32	40	—
8	.1640	32	36	—
10	.1900	24	32	—
12	.2160	24	28	32
1/4	.2500	20	28	32
5/16	.3125	18	24	32
3/8	.3750	16	24	32
7/16	.4375	14	20	28
1/2	.5000	13	20	28
9/16	.5625	12	18	24
5/8	.6250	11	18	24
11/16	.6875	—	—	24
3/4	.7500	10	16	20
13/16	.8125	—	—	20
7/8	.8750	9	14	20
15/16	.9275	—	—	20
1	1.0000	8	12	20
1 1/8	1.1250	7	12	18
1 1/4	1.2500	7	12	18

*The major diameter is the outside diameter of the screw thread.

MACHINE BOLTS

Machine bolts are specified by size, number of threads per inch, material, type of head and length. Example: ⅜-16 steel hex-head machine bolt, 2″ long. Note that the length is measured from the end of the bolt to the underside of the head. See Standard Machine Threads on page 157 for thread options.

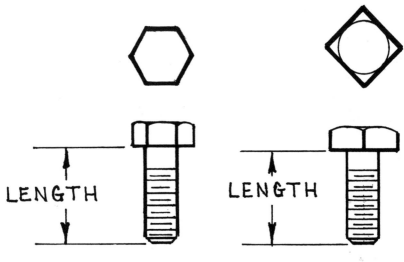

Hex-head Machine Bolt   Square-head Machine Bolt

MACHINE SCREWS

Machine screws are specified by size, number of threads per inch, material, type of head and the length. Example: 10-32 brass ovalhead machine screw, 1½″ long. See Standard Machine Threads on page 157 for thread options.

Screw head options are shown below: (A) flathead, (B) roundhead, (C) ovalhead, (D) fillister head, (E) hex-head and (F) socket head.

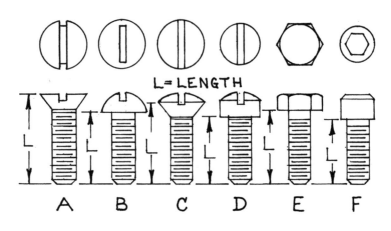

HANGER BOLTS

Usually available only in steel.

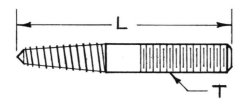

COMMONLY AVAILABLE SIZES

THREAD (T)	LENGTH (L) (inches)	THREAD (T)	LENGTH (L) (inches)
10-24	1	$5/16$-18	$2\frac{1}{2}$
10-24	$1\frac{1}{2}$	$5/16$-18	3
10-24	$1\frac{3}{4}$	$5/16$-18	$3\frac{1}{2}$
10-24	2	$5/16$-18	4
10-24	3	$5/16$-18	$4\frac{1}{2}$
10-24	$3\frac{1}{2}$	$5/16$-18	5
$1/4$-20	$1\frac{1}{2}$	$5/16$-18	$5\frac{1}{2}$
$1/4$-20	$1\frac{3}{4}$	$5/16$-18	6
$1/4$-20	2	$3/8$-16	2
$1/4$-20	$2\frac{1}{4}$	$3/8$-16	$2\frac{1}{2}$
$1/4$-20	$2\frac{1}{2}$	$3/8$-16	3
$1/4$-20	$2\frac{3}{4}$	$3/8$-16	$3\frac{1}{2}$
$1/4$-20	3	$3/8$-16	4
$1/4$-20	$3\frac{1}{2}$	$3/8$-16	$4\frac{1}{2}$
$1/4$-20	4	$3/8$-16	5
$1/4$-20	5	$3/8$-16	$5\frac{1}{2}$
$5/16$-18	2	$3/8$-16	6

DOWEL SCREWS

Usually available only in steel.

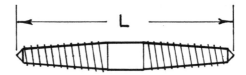

COMMONLY AVAILABLE SIZES

SIZE	LENGTH (L) (inches)	SIZE	LENGTH (L) (inches)
Number 10	1½	¼	3½
³⁄₁₆	1½	⁵⁄₁₆	1½
³⁄₁₆	1¾	⁵⁄₁₆	2
³⁄₁₆	2	⁵⁄₁₆	2½
³⁄₁₆	2½	⁵⁄₁₆	3
³⁄₁₆	3	⁵⁄₁₆	3½
¼	1½	⁵⁄₁₆	4
¼	1¾	⁵⁄₁₆	4½
¼	2	⁵⁄₁₆	5
¼	2½	³⁄₈	5½
¼	3	³⁄₈	6

LAG SCREWS

Available in steel with either square head or hex head. Also, available in stainless steel in some sizes and lengths.

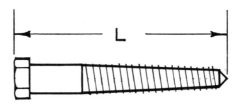

LAG SCREWS—COMMONLY AVAILABLE SIZES

SIZE	LENGTH (L) (inches)	SIZE	LENGTH (L) (inches)
¼	1	½	1½
¼	1¼	½	1¾
¼	1½	½	2
¼	1¾	½	2½
¼	2	½	3
¼	2½	½	3½
¼	3	½	4
¼	3½	½	4½
¼	4	½	5
¼	4½	½	6
¼	5	½	6½
¼	5½	½	7
¼	6	½	8
⁵⁄₁₆	1	½	9
⁵⁄₁₆	1¼	½	10
⁵⁄₁₆	1½	½	12
⁵⁄₁₆	1¾		
⁵⁄₁₆	2	⅝	2
⁵⁄₁₆	2½	⅝	2½
⁵⁄₁₆	3	⅝	3
⁵⁄₁₆	3½	⅝	3½
⁵⁄₁₆	4	⅝	4
⁵⁄₁₆	4½	⅝	4½
⁵⁄₁₆	5	⅝	5
⁵⁄₁₆	6	⅝	5½
⅜	1	⅝	6
⅜	1¼	⅝	7
⅜	1½	⅝	8
⅜	1¾	⅝	10
⅜	2	⅝	12
⅜	2½	¾	2½
⅜	3	¾	3
⅜	3½	¾	3½
⅜	4	¾	4
⅜	4½	¾	4½
⅜	5	¾	5
⅜	5½	¾	5½
⅜	6	¾	6
⅜	6½	¾	7
⅜	7	¾	8
⅜	8	¾	10
⅜	10	¾	12

CARRIAGE BOLTS

(SQUARE NECKED)

Available in steel. Also available in stainless steel in some sizes and lengths.

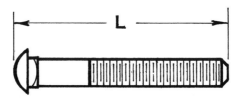

COMMONLY AVAILABLE SIZES

SIZE	LENGTH (L) (inches)	SIZE	LENGTH (L) (inches)
$\frac{1}{4}$-20	1	$\frac{3}{8}$-16	$1\frac{1}{2}$
$\frac{1}{4}$-20	$1\frac{1}{4}$	$\frac{3}{8}$-16	$1\frac{3}{4}$
$\frac{1}{4}$-20	$1\frac{1}{2}$	$\frac{3}{8}$-16	2
$\frac{1}{4}$-20	$1\frac{3}{4}$	$\frac{3}{8}$-16	$2\frac{1}{2}$
$\frac{1}{4}$-20	2	$\frac{3}{8}$-16	3
$\frac{1}{4}$-20	$2\frac{1}{2}$	$\frac{3}{8}$-16	$3\frac{1}{2}$
$\frac{1}{4}$-20	3	$\frac{3}{8}$-16	4
$\frac{1}{4}$-20	$3\frac{1}{2}$	$\frac{3}{8}$-16	$4\frac{1}{2}$
$\frac{1}{4}$-20	4	$\frac{3}{8}$-16	5
$\frac{1}{4}$-20	$4\frac{1}{2}$	$\frac{3}{8}$-16	$5\frac{1}{2}$
$\frac{1}{4}$-20	5	$\frac{3}{8}$-16	6
$\frac{1}{4}$-20	6	$\frac{1}{2}$-13	$1\frac{1}{2}$
$\frac{5}{16}$-18	1	$\frac{1}{2}$-13	2
$\frac{5}{16}$-18	$1\frac{1}{4}$	$\frac{1}{2}$-13	$2\frac{1}{2}$
$\frac{5}{16}$-18	$1\frac{1}{2}$	$\frac{1}{2}$-13	3
$\frac{5}{16}$-18	2	$\frac{1}{2}$-13	$3\frac{1}{2}$
$\frac{5}{16}$-18	$2\frac{1}{2}$	$\frac{1}{2}$-13	4
$\frac{5}{16}$-18	3	$\frac{1}{2}$-13	$4\frac{1}{2}$
$\frac{5}{16}$-18	$3\frac{1}{2}$	$\frac{1}{2}$-13	5
$\frac{5}{16}$-18	4	$\frac{1}{2}$-13	$5\frac{1}{2}$
$\frac{5}{16}$-18	$4\frac{1}{2}$	$\frac{1}{2}$-13	6
$\frac{5}{16}$-18	5	$\frac{1}{2}$-13	$6\frac{1}{2}$
$\frac{5}{16}$-18	6	$\frac{1}{2}$-13	7
$\frac{3}{8}$-16	1	$\frac{1}{2}$-13	8

BRADS

Brad sizes are designated by length and wire gauge number.

COMMONLY AVAILABLE SIZES

LENGTH (inches)	WIRE GAUGE Number	LENGTH (inches)	WIRE GAUGE Number
½	19	1	16
½	20	1	17
⅝	18	1	18
⅝	19	1¼	15
¾	16	1¼	16
¾	17	1¼	17
¾	18	1¼	18
⅞	17	1½	16
⅞	18	1½	17

PLAIN WASHER DIMENSIONS
(FOR LAG SCREWS AND BOLTS)

Washers are made from steel.

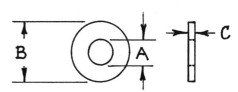

LAG SCREW OR BOLT SIZE (inches)	HOLE DIAMETER (A) (inches)	OUTSIDE DIAMETER (B) (inches)	THICKNESS (C) (inches)
³/₁₆	¼	⁹/₁₆	³/₆₄
¼	⁵/₁₆	¾	¹/₁₆
⁵/₁₆	⅜	⅞	¹/₁₆
⅜	⁷/₁₆	1	⁵/₆₄
⁷/₁₆	½	1¼	⁵/₆₄
½	⁹/₁₆	1⅜	³/₃₂
⁹/₁₆	⅝	1½	³/₃₂
⅝	¹¹/₁₆	1¾	⅛
¾	¹³/₁₆	2	⅛

COMMON BUTT HINGE SIZES

Butt hinges come in a wide range of sizes. Some of the commonly available ones are shown here.

Butt hinge sizes are specified by their length (L) and open width (W). For example, a 2×3 butt hinge has a length of 2″ and a width (with the leaves open) of 3″.

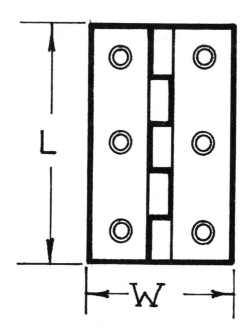

LENGTH	WIDTH	LENGTH	WIDTH
½	½	1½	1¼
½	⁹⁄₁₆	1½	2
¾	½	1½	2⅜
¾	1	2	⅞
¾	⅝	2	1
1	⅝	2	1⅛
1	¾	2	1¼
1	1	2	1⅜
1¼	⅝	2	3
1¼	¾	2¼	1¼
1¼	1⅞	2½	1⅜
1½	¾	2½	1½
1½	⅞	2½	1⅝
1½	1	3	1⅝
1½	1½	3	2

KNOCK-DOWN HARDWARE

THREADED INSERTS (ROSAN NUTS)

Usually available in brass or steel.

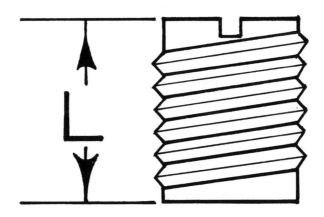

COMMONLY AVAILABLE SIZES

INTERNAL THREAD	LENGTH (L) (inches)	INTERNAL THREAD	LENGTH (L) (inches)
4-40	³⁄₈	¹⁄₄-28	¹⁄₂
6-32	³⁄₈	⁵⁄₁₆-18	⁵⁄₈
8-32	³⁄₈	⁵⁄₁₆-24	⁵⁄₈
10-24	¹⁄₂	³⁄₈-16	⁵⁄₈
10-32	¹⁄₂	³⁄₈-24	⁵⁄₈
¹⁄₄-20	¹⁄₂		

TEE-NUTS

Usually available in steel or plated steel.

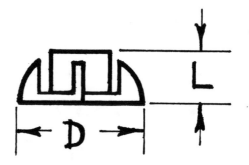

COMMONLY AVAILABLE SIZES

INTERNAL THREAD	FLANGE DIAMETER (D) (inches)	BARREL LENGTH (L) (inches)
4-40	$^3/_8$	$^7/_{64}$
6-32	$^9/_{16}$	$^1/_4$
8-32	$^{23}/_{32}$	$^1/_4$
10-24	$^3/_4$	$^5/_{16}$
$^1/_4$-20	$^3/_4$	$^5/_{16}$
$^1/_4$-20	$^3/_4$	$^9/_{16}$
$^5/_{16}$-18	$^7/_8$	$^3/_8$
$^3/_8$-16	1	$^7/_{16}$

CHAPTER 9

FINISHING

COATED ABRASIVES

Coated abrasives include such products as sheet sandpaper, belt sander belts, bench sander belts, sanding disks and more. Coated abrasive products vary depending upon the size and type of abrasive particle, the type of backing and also the kind of adhesive that is used to bond the particles to the backing. Much of the coated abrasive information included here is courtesy of the Norton Abrasive Company.

COATED ABRASIVE PARTICLE SIZES

Coated abrasives are graded according to the size of the particles (also called grits or grains). In the United States, sandpaper manufacturers adhere to the grading specifications of the Coated Abrasive Manufacturers Institute (CAMI). Most European sandpaper manufacturers, and some U.S. manufacturers, use the grading specifications of the Federation of European Producers of Abrasives (FEPA). FEPA sandpaper particle sizes are prefixed by the letter P. Sandpaper made from emery has a unique grading system.

Use this chart to convert or compare the CAMI, FEPA and emery grading systems. The chart also provides the particle size both in inches and microns. A micron, by the way, is equal to one millionth of a meter.

PARTICLE SIZE (inches)	PARTICLE SIZE (microns)	ALL PRODUCTS OTHER THAN EMERY—GRADING SYSTEM		EMERY	
		CAMI	FEPA	Polishing Paper	Cloth
.00026	6.5	1200	—	4/0	—
.00036	9.2	1000	—	2/0	—
.00048	12.2	800	—	—	—
.00060	15.3	—	P1200	—	—
.00062	16.0	600	—	1/0	—
.00071	18.3	—	P1000	—	—
.00077	19.7	500	—	0	—
.00085	21.8	—	P800	—	—
.00092	23.6	400	—	—	—
.00100	25.75	—	P600	—	—
.00112	28.8	360	—	—	—
.00118	30.0	—	P500	—	—
.00137	35.0	—	P400	—	—
.00140	36.0	320	—	—	—
.00158	40.5	—	P360	—	—
.00172	44.0	280	—	1	—

PARTICLE SIZE (inches)	PARTICLE SIZE (microns)	ALL PRODUCTS OTHER THAN EMERY—GRADING SYSTEM		EMERY	
		CAMI	FEPA	Polishing Paper	Cloth
.00180	46.2	—	P320	—	—
.00204	52.5	—	P280	—	—
.00209	53.5	240	—	—	—
.00228	58.5	—	P240	—	—
.00254	65.0	—	P220	—	—
.00257	66.0	220	—	2	—
.00304	78.0	180	P180	3	—
.00363	93.0	150	—	—	Fine
.00378	97.0	—	P150	—	—
.00452	116.0	120	—	—	—
.00495	127.0	—	P120	—	—
.00550	141.0	100	—	—	Medium
.00608	156.0	—	P100	—	—
.00749	192.0	80	—	—	Coarse
.00768	197.0	—	P80	—	—
.01014	260.0	—	P60	—	—
.01045	268.0	60	—	—	—
.01271	326.0	—	P50	—	—
.01369	351.0	50	—	—	Ex-Coarse
.01601	412.0	—	P40	—	—
.01669	428.0	40	—	—	—
.02044	524.0	—	P36	—	—
.02087	535.0	36	—	—	—
.02426	622.0	—	P30	—	—
.02448	638.0	30	—	—	—
.02789	715.0	24	—	—	—
.02886	740.0	—	P24	—	—
.03530	905.0	20	—	—	—
.03838	984.0	—	P20	—	—
.05148	1320.0	16	—	—	—
.05164	1324.0	—	P16	—	—
.06880	1764.0	—	P12	—	—
.07184	1842.0	12	—	—	—

ABRASIVE MATERIALS

Several man-made and natural materials are used to make abrasive particles. The most commonly used abrasive materials are described here.

MATERIAL	DESCRIPTION
Aluminum oxide	Man-made abrasive. Extremely tough. Well suited for hardwoods, carbon steel, alloy steels and bronze.
Silicon carbide	Man-made abrasive. Hardest and sharpest of the commonly used abrasive materials, although it tends to be brittle. Generally used for finishing non-ferrous metals (aluminum, brass, bronze, etc.), plastics, rubber, softwoods and hardwoods.
Zirconia alumina	Man-made abrasive. Has long life because abrasive particles self-sharpen in use. Often used for heavy wood sanding and metal grinding applications.
Garnet	Natural abrasive. Not as hard or durable as the man-made abrasives. Particles have sharp edges but tend to dull rapidly when used to sand metal. Often used for finish sanding of furniture and wood products.
Emery	Natural abrasive. Blocky-shaped particles cut slowly. Used primarily for polishing metals.
Flint	Natural abrasive. Tends to dull quickly. Low cost often makes it the best choice for applications that cause sandpaper to clog quickly, such as removing paint or old finish.

BACKINGS FOR COATED ABRASIVES

Several types of backing material are used to make coated abrasives, but paper or cloth backings are used most often for woodworking applications.

Paper Backing
Paper backing is classified by weight. (Paper weights are based on the number of pounds in a ream of 480 sheets.) Lighter-weight backing offers greater flexibility; heavier-weight backing provides better resistance to tearing. Some paper backings are waterproofed to permit use in wet applications.

Cloth Backing
Compared to paper backings, cloth backings offer better durability and resistance to tearing, plus they stand up better to constant flexing when in use.

PAPER BACKING

WEIGHT	DESCRIPTION
A-weight	Made from 40-pound paper. Light and flexible. Used mostly for hand finishing work.
C-weight	Made from 70-pound paper. Less flexible, but stronger than A-weight backing. Used for hand sanding work and with small portable power sanders.
D-weight	Made from 90-pound paper. Less flexible, but stronger than C-weight backing. Used for hand sanding work and with small portable power sanders.
E-weight	Made from 130-pound paper. Less flexible, but stronger than D-weight backing. Used when high resistance to tearing is important, such as roll, belt and disc sander applications.
F-weight	Made from 165-pound paper. Least flexible, but strongest weight. Mostly used for rolls and belts in industrial applications.

CLOTH BACKING

WEIGHT	DESCRIPTION
J-weight (Jeans)	Lightest and most flexible cloth backing. Typically used to sand curved surfaces.
X-weight (Drills)	Less flexible, but stronger than J-weight backing. Used for applications ranging from coarse-grit heavy sanding through fine-grit polishing.
Y-weight (Heavy Drills or Sateen)	Stronger, with better resistance to longitudinal splitting than regular drills cloth. Used in severe applications such as narrow belt grinding of hand tools and wide belt sanding of wood and particleboard.
H-weight (Heavy Duty)	Strongest cloth backing. Use for applications requiring coarse grits and heavy stock removal.

Note: In addition to those shown here, a few other cloth backings are sometimes used. They include combination backing (a lamination of paper and cloth), fiber backing, and polyester film backing.

COAT COVERAGE

The amount of abrasive particles applied to the backing is called the coverage. There are two coverage options: open coat and closed coat.

COVERAGE	DESCRIPTION
Closed coat	Abrasive particles completely cover the surface. Removes a lot of material before dulling.
Open coat	Abrasive particles cover about 50 to 60 percent of the surface. Tends to cut fast with a minimum of clogging. Better flexibility than closed coat.

ADHESIVE BONDS

Abrasive particles are bonded to the backing with an adhesive. Two types of adhesive are used to bond abrasives: animal glue and resin-based glue. Two coats of the adhesive are applied. A "maker" coat is added first, followed by a "sizer" coat.

ADHESIVE BOND	DESCRIPTION
Glue	Uses animal hide glue for both the maker and sizer coat. Produces more uniform, less harsh finish.
Resin	Liquid phenolic or urea adhesive product. Used for both maker and sizer coat. Offers greater durability and resistance to heat when removing heavy amounts of material. Best all-around adhesive for coated abrasives.
Resin over glue	Resin sizer coat added over glue maker coat to combine the advantages of each bond. Cuts faster than glue bond, yet results in a better finish than resin bond.

SANDPAPER USE CHART

GRIT SIZE	TYPICAL USES
24 to 36	Removing heavy paint and finishes.
40 to 50	Smoothing very rough wood surfaces. Removing paint and heavy finishes.
60 to 80	Preliminary sanding of rough wood. Removing planer marks.
100 to 120	Smoothing wood surfaces. Removing scratches from the 60-80 grit sanding step.
150 to 180	Removing scratches from the 100-120 grit step.
220 to 240	Final sanding of wood surfaces.
280 to 320	Sanding between finish coats.
360 to 400	Final sanding of finish coat.

STEEL WOOL GRADES

GRADE NUMBER	DESCRIPTION	TYPICAL USE
4	Extra coarse	Removing chipped paint and heavy rust
3	Coarse	Removing paint and heavy rust
2	Medium coarse	Removing paint and rust
1	Medium	Smoothing wood scratches; removing raised wood fibers
0 (1/0)	Fine	Smoothing shallow wood scratches; removing raised wood fibers; stripping finishes
00 (2/0)	Very fine	Light smoothing between finish coats
000 (3/0)	Extra fine	Smoothing between finish coats
0000 (4/0)	Super fine	Final rub down of finish

THINNING SHELLAC

The term "pound cut" describes the number of pounds of shellac flakes in a gallon of alcohol solvent. For example, a 3-pound cut has three pounds of shellac flakes in one gallon of alcohol. When shellac needs to be thinned to a lower pound cut, use this chart as a guide for adding the correct amount of alcohol.

STARTING POUND CUT	DESIRED POUND CUT	MIXING PROPORTIONS	
		Alcohol	Shellac
5	4	1 part	4 parts
5	3	1 part	2 parts
5	2	1 part	1 part
5	1	2 parts	1 part
5	½	7 parts	1 part
4	3	1 part	4 parts
4	2	3 parts	4 parts
4	1	3 parts	1 part
4	½	5 parts	1 part
3	2	2 parts	5 parts
3	1	4 parts	3 parts
3	½	4 parts	1 part

CHOOSING A STAIN

Pigment stains consist of finely ground particles suspended in a water- or oil-based solvent. When applied to wood the solvent evaporates, leaving the colored pigment on the wood surface. Pigment stains are relatively easy to use and are available in a wide choice of colors, but they tend to obscure the grain of the wood somewhat.

Aniline dye powders dissolve completely when mixed with water-, alcohol- or oil-based solvents. The dissolved dyes thoroughly saturate the wood fibers with color, allowing the grain to show through.

STAIN TYPE	FORM	PREPARATION	CHARACTERISTICS
Pigment Stains			
Oil-based	Liquid	Mix thoroughly	Apply with rag, brush or spray; resists fading.
Water-based	Liquid	Mix thoroughly	Apply with rag, brush or spray; resists fading; water cleanup.
Gel	Gel	Ready to use	Apply with rag; won't raise grain; easy to use; no drips or runs.
Water-based gel	Gel	Ready to use	Apply with rag; easy to use; no drips or runs; water cleanup.
Japan color	Concentrated liquid	Mix thoroughly	Used for tinting stains, paints, varnish, lacquer.
Dye Stains			
Water-based	Powder	Mix with water	Apply with rag, brush or spray; deep penetrating; best fade resistance of dye stains; good clarity; raises grain.
Oil-based	Powder	Mix with toluol, lacquer thinner, turpentine or naphtha	Apply with rag, brush or spray; penetrating; does not raise grain; dries slowly.
Alcohol-based	Powder	Mix with alcohol	Apply with rag, brush or spray; penetrating, does not raise grain; dries quickly; lap marks sometimes a problem.
NGR	Liquid	Mix thoroughly	Apply with rag, brush or spray (use retarder if wiping or brushing); good clarity; does not raise grain.

CHOOSING A TOPCOAT

FINISH TYPE	FORM	PREPARATION	CHARACTERISTICS
Shellac	Liquid	Mix thoroughly	Dries quickly; economical; available either clear or amber-colored; high gloss luster; affected by water, alcohol and heat.
Shellac flakes	Dry flakes	Mix with alcohol	Dries quickly; economical (mix only what is needed); color choices from amber to clear; high gloss luster; affected by water, alcohol and heat.
Lacquer	Liquid	Mix with thinner for spraying	Dries quickly; clear (shaded lacquers available), high gloss luster, but flattening agents available; durable; moisture resistant.
Varnish	Liquid	Mix thoroughly	Dries slowly; amber color; gloss, semi-gloss or satin lusters; very good durability and moisture resistance; flexible.
Polyurethane	Liquid	Mix thoroughly	Dries slowly; clear to amber colors; gloss, semi-gloss and satin lusters; excellent durability and moisture resistance; flexible.
Water-based polyurethane	Liquid	Mix thoroughly	Dries quickly; clear; won't yellow; gloss and satin lusters; moisture and alcohol resistant; low odor.
Tung oil	Liquid	Ready to use	Dries slowly; amber color; satin luster; poor moisture resistance; easy to use.
Danish oil	Liquid	Mix thoroughly	Dries slowly; amber color; satin luster; poor moisture resistance; easy to use.

TOPCOAT DRY TIMES

FINISH TYPE	DRY TIME
Shellac	2 hours
Lacquer	30 minutes
Varnish	3 to 6 hours
Polyurethane	3 to 6 hours
Water-based polyurethane	2 hours
Tung oil	20 to 24 hours
Danish oil	8 to 10 hours

Note: Dry times are based on a temperature of 70° Fahrenheit and 40 percent relative humidity. Lower temperature and/or higher relative humidity can increase drying time.

MAKING A TACK RAG

1. Use mineral spirits to dampen a piece of cheesecloth or cotton cloth.
2. Place the cloth in a resealable plastic bag and add a small amount of varnish to the cloth. Close the bag.
3. Knead the cloth in the bag until the entire cloth surface becomes moderately sticky.
4. Store the tack rag in the plastic bag (or in a glass jar). Over a period of time, the rag is going to dry and lose some stickiness, but it can be rejuvenated simply by adding a bit more varnish.

CHAPTER 10

SAFETY

GENERAL SAFETY RULES

The workshop is a great place to relax and enjoy working with wood, but it is not without hazards. Cutters and blades revolving at high speed can inflict serious injury—even death. A misused hand chisel can cause nasty cuts. A flying chip from the table saw can permanently injure an unprotected eye.

Clearly, it's important to use a good measure of caution and common sense when in the workshop. To that end, I suggest that you photocopy these rules and post them in a conspicuous place in your workshop. If you keep these do's and don'ts in mind, your workshop will be a safer place.

Do install a smoke detector in the workshop.

Do keep a class ABC fire extinguisher in the workshop.

Do wear safety glasses in the workshop. Wear goggles when using chemicals or finishes that are dangerous to eyes.

Do wear hearing protection when using noisy power equipment.

Don't attempt any procedure that makes you concerned about safety.

Don't attempt any procedure unless properly equipped.

Don't work when tired or under the influence of medication, alcohol or drugs.

Do be sure to know your power tool—read the owner's manual and understand the limitations and potential hazards of the tool before using it.

Do keep cutting tool edges properly sharpened.

Do use blade guards on tools that are equipped with them.

Do use power tools that are double-insulated and grounded.

Don't use power tools in wet locations.

Do unplug power tools before making adjustments or changing sawblades, bits, cutters and the like.

(Continued on next page)

GENERAL SAFETY RULES (CONT'D)

Do make sure that the power tool switch is in the "off" position before connecting the power plug.

Don't force a tool to do an operation that it's not designed to do.

Do use clamps or other means to make sure that the workpiece is held securely in place when using a power tool.

Do keep hands well away from moving saw blades, bits, cutters and the like.

Don't wear jewelry or loose clothing that can get caught in moving parts.

Do wear a dust mask if the work is producing dust.

Do keep the workshop clean and uncluttered.

Do keep the workshop well lighted.

Don't allow children near the work area.

Do use a NIOSH (National Institute for Occupational Safety and Health) approved dual-cartridge respirator when using chemicals, finishes or solvents that produce hazardous vapors. Install filters that are appropriate for the chemicals or finishes used.

Do provide adequate ventilation when using chemicals, finishes or solvents that produce hazardous vapors.

Do place all oily waste materials in a sealed water-filled metal container to avoid the dangers of spontaneous combustion.

Do store flammables in a metal container away from sources of ignition or heat.

Don't use solvents like acetone, mineral spirits or lacquer thinner to clean your hands—the solvents can be absorbed into the body through the skin.

Do not smoke, drink or eat when using chemicals, finishes or solvents.

Do dispose of chemicals, finishes or solvents in an environmentally friendly manner. Don't dump them onto the ground or down drains.

SAFE EXTENSION CORD LENGTHS

An extension cord with a wire gauge size that's too small causes a drop in voltage, loss of power, motor overheating and possible motor damage. Use this chart as a guide to selecting the correct wire gauge size based on the motor ampere rating and the extension cord length. (The smaller the wire gauge size, the larger the wire diameter.) The chart is based on limiting the line voltage drop to five volts at 150 percent of the rated amps. The wire gauge sizes shown are American Wire Gauge (AWG). If the tool is to be used outdoors, you must use an extension cord rated for outdoor service.

Example 1: An electric drill has a 3.5 amp motor. The drill needs a 75′ extension cord in order to reach a backyard shed. What's the minimum wire gauge size that can be used with the 3.5 amp motor?
Answer: Referring to the chart, a minimum wire gauge of 16 must be used.

Example 2: A belt sander with a 7.5 amp motor requires a 50′ extension cord. What's the minimum wire gauge size that can be used?
Answer: Referring to the chart, a minimum wire gauge of 14 must be used.

TOOL AMPERE RATING (shown on nameplate)	MINIMUM WIRE GAUGE SIZE (AWG)			
	25′	50′	75′	100′
0–2.0	18	18	18	18
2.1–3.4	18	18	18	16
3.5–5.0	18	18	16	14
5.1–7.0	18	16	14	12
7.1–12.0	16	14	12	10

NOISE IN THE WORKSHOP

Noise is defined as any unwanted sound. Some sounds, unfortunately, have such high intensity that they can cause permanent hearing loss. The Occupational Safety and Health Administration (OSHA) has set standards for limiting worker exposure to dangerous noise levels.

Sound, including noise, is measured using a unit called the decibel (dB). The decibel level for an assortment of sounds, including several woodworking power tools, is shown on the next page (see Noise Levels of Various Sounds on page 183).

Noise danger is related not only to the intensity of the sound, but also to the length of time that you are exposed to a sound (see Permissible Noise Exposure Time).

Based on an eight-hour day, OSHA has determined that a decibel level greater than 90 can cause hearing loss. (Some experts feel that number should be lowered to 85 decibels.) As shown in the chart, most woodworking power tools exceed the 90 decibel limit, so be sure to wear ear protection when running woodworking equipment. A good set of ear plugs or earmuff-type hearing protectors, properly fitted and used, can reduce noise levels by 15 to 30 decibels, depending upon the manufacturer and model. Make sure, however, that the 15 to 30 decibel drop lowers the noise to a safe level.

For more information about noise and its effects on hearing loss, contact the National Institute for Occupational Safety and Health (part of the U.S. Department of Health and Human Services); tel. (800) 35-NIOSH.

PERMISSIBLE NOISE EXPOSURE TIME

Use this chart to determine the maximum length of time that you can be safely exposed to various noise levels.

Example: A radial arm saw creates 105 decibels of noise as it cuts dadoes in wide stock. How long can you continue routing before it becomes a risk to your hearing?

Answer: As shown in the chart, at a noise level of 105 decibels, the exposure time must be limited to a maximum of one hour.

Note: If you wear ear protectors that reduce the noise level by 15 decibels (from 105 dB to 90 dB), you can increase the maximum exposure time to 8 hours.

NOISE LEVEL (dB)	TIME LIMIT PER DAY (hours)	NOISE LEVEL (dB)	TIME LIMIT PER DAY (hours)
115	¼ or less	100	2
110	½	97	3
107	¾	95	4
105	1	92	6
102	1½	90	8

NOISE LEVELS OF VARIOUS SOUNDS

Keep in mind that this scale is logarithmic, not linear. A 95 dB noise has one hundred times more sound energy than a 75 dB noise. All the woodworking power tool measurements are taken from the normal position of the machine operator. The decibel levels represent the noise generated when the tool is cutting (or sanding) wood. The decibel levels shown are approximate and can vary somewhat depending on room size, specific machine type and other factors.

WOODWORKING POWER TOOLS	DECIBEL LEVEL (dB)	OTHER SOUNDS
	150	Jet taking off (150)
	145	
	140	Gunshot (140)
	135	
	130	Jackhammer (130)
	125	
	120	Rock concert (120)
	115	
Chain saw (108)	110	Textile loom (110)
Radial-arm saw (105)	105	
Portable circular saw (100)	100	
Router (95), Belt sander (93)	95	
Planer (93), Table saw (92)	90	Law mower (90)
Drill press (85)	85	
	80	Subway (80)
	75	
	70	Busy street (70)
	65	
	60	Restaurant (60)
	55	
	50	Conversation (50)
	45	
	40	Urban home (40)
	35	
	30	Suburban home (30)
	25	
	20	Whisper (20)
	15	
	10	Rustling leaves (10)
	5	
	0	Silence

WORKING WITH PRESSURE-TREATED WOOD

Since the advent of pressure-treated lumber, billions of board feet have been safely used. However, be aware that to make the lumber resistant to moisture and insects, the pressure-treating process forces chemicals deep into the wood cells (see page 85). The pressure-treated lumber commonly used for backyard decks contains the chemicals chromated copper arsenate (CCA) or ammoniacal copper zinc arsenate (ACZA). Both of these chemicals contain inorganic arsenic, so it certainly is prudent to follow some special safety rules when working with pressure-treated lumber.

SAFETY RULES FOR WORKING WITH PRESSURE-TREATED LUMBER

Always wear a dust mask.

Always wear gloves when handling pressure-treated lumber (unless the gloves pose a risk when using power equipment).

After construction, sawdust from pressure-treated wood should be cleaned up and properly disposed.

Clothes covered with pressure-treated sawdust should be washed separately from other household clothing.

Don't use pressure-treated wood where the chemical could become a component of food or animal feed.

Don't use pressure-treated wood where it could come into direct or indirect contact with drinking water (except incidental contact such as when used on docks or bridges).

Don't use pressure-treated wood to make toys, countertops or kitchen cutting boards.

Don't burn pressure-treated wood because toxic chemicals could be produced as part of the smoke and ashes.

HAZARDOUS WOODWORKING CHEMICALS

Many commonly used workshop products contain hazardous chemicals. Such products as adhesives, degreasers, thinners, solvents, dyes, fillers, strippers, stains, waxes and finishes often include chemicals that could pose a threat to your health if not used with caution. Also, many workshop chemicals are a dangerous fire hazard when exposed to heat or flames.

Exposure to chemicals can produce both acute and chronic effects. Acute effects generally result from single short-term exposures, usually less than twenty-four hours in duration. Chronic effects generally result from long and repeated exposures, often in small amounts, usually over a period of time greater than a few months.

Hazardous chemicals can enter the body through inhalation, ingestion and skin contact. Many woodworking-related chemicals quickly become vapors, so inhalation is a common route of entry into the body. Always use a well-fitting respirator approved by the National Institute for Occupational Safety and Health (NIOSH), and be sure that the filter is acceptable for the chemical in use. For some chemicals, like methylene chloride and methanol, there is no approved filter. Also, remember that filters have a limited life span, so they must be changed periodically.

Ingestion can occur when a chemical is accidentally swallowed, an unfortunate event that happens to children more than adults. Adults are more likely to ingest chemicals by bringing food, drink or cigarettes into the shop. Indeed, vapors can settle on food and drink, which soon end up in the stomach to be absorbed by the bloodstream. Also, vapors that settle on hands can easily be transferred to a cigarette and then to the mouth. To avoid ingesting chemicals, don't eat, drink or smoke in the shop. Of course, smoking also increases the risk of fire when using chemicals that are flammable.

Some chemicals can be absorbed through the skin or through skin cuts and abrasions. The chemicals are then absorbed by the blood. To minimize this risk, always wear approved gloves when handling chemical products. And, be sure to wash hands thoroughly with soap and water after working.

The list that follows includes many of the chemicals commonly found in woodshop products. The list describes the dangers presented by the chemical and notes the Threshold Limit Value (TLV). The TLV represents the maximum airborne contaminant level, in parts per million (ppm), that most healthy adults can be exposed to in a forty-hour work week without a health risk. The lower the TLV, the more dangerous the chemical.

ACETONE

Synonyms: Dimethyl ketone, ketone propane, propanone, pyroacetic ether
Common uses: Epoxy, lacquer, paint stripper, wood filler
Toxicity (TLV in ppm): 750
Dangers: Can irritate eyes, nose, throat, skin and central nervous system; high vapor
    levels can cause narcosis
Fire risk: Extremely flammable

BENZENE

Synonyms: Benzol, coal naphtha, carbon oil, cyclohezatriene
Common uses: Lacquer thinner, petroleum distillate, paint stripper
Toxicity (TLV in ppm): 10
Dangers: Do not use; dangerous carcinogen; can poison through inhalation of the
    vapors or absorption through skin; chronic exposure may cause leukemia
Fire risk: Extremely flammable

BIS(2,3-EPOXYPROPYL) ETHER

(see Digylcidyl ether)

BUTYL METHYL KETONE

(see Methyl n-butyl ketone)

CARBON OIL

(see Benzene)

COAL NAPHTHA

(see Benzene)

CYCLOHEZATRIENE

(see Benzene)

DGE

(see Digylcidyl ether)

DIALLYL ETHER DIOXIDE

(see Digylcidyl ether)

DICHLOROMETHANE

(see Methylene chloride)

DI(EPOXYPROPYL) ETHER
(see Digylcidyl ether)

DIGYLCIDYL ETHER
Synonyms: Bis(2,3-epoxypropyl) ether, DGE, diallyl ether dioxide, di(epoxypropyl)
     ether, 2,3-epoxypropyl ether
Common uses: Epoxy
Toxicity (TLV in ppm): 0.1
Dangers: Can cause severe irritation of skin, eyes and respiratory system; skin burns

DIMETHYL BENZENE
(see Xylene)

2,3-EPOXYPROPYL ETHER
(see Digylcidyl ether)

ESANI
(see n-Hexane)

ETHANOL
Synonyms: Ethyl alcohol, methyl carbinol, wood alcohol
Common uses: Shellac, stain
Toxicity (TLV in ppm): 1,000
Dangers: Can affect eyes, nose, skin, central nervous system and upper respiratory
     tract; large doses can cause alcohol poisoning
Fire risk: Dangerous when exposed to heat or flame

ETHYL ALCOHOL
(see Ethanol)

GUM SPIRITS
(see Turpentine)

GUM TURPENTINE
(see Turpentine)

HEKSAN
(see n-Hexane)

N-HEXANE
Synonyms: Esani, heksan, hexanen
Common uses: Contact cement, quick-drying cement, rubber cement, rubbing oils,
     spray adhesive, varnish
Toxicity (TLV in ppm): 50
Dangers: Can affect skin, respiratory system, central and peripheral nervous systems,
     general health
Fire risk: Dangerous when exposed to heat, flame and powerful oxidizers

HEXANEN
(see n-Hexane)

2-HEXANONE
(see Methyl n-butyl ketone)

HEXONE
(see Methyl-isobutyl ketone)

ISOBUTYL METHYL KETONE
(see Methyl-isobutyl ketone)

ISOPROPYL ALCOHOL
Synonyms: Isopropanol, rubbing alcohol
Common uses: Lacquer
Toxicity (TLV in ppm): 400
Dangers: Can cause irritation of eyes and skin; high airborne concentrations may
     cause narcosis

KETONE PROPANE
(see Acetone)

KSYLEN
(see Xylene)

MBK
(see Methyl n-butyl ketone)

METHANOL
Synonyms: Carbinol, methyl alcohol, wood alcohol, wood spirit
Common uses: Dye, lacquer, paint, paint stripper, varnish
Toxicity (TLV in ppm): 200
Dangers: Can affect skin, eyes, central nervous system; ingestion may cause blindness
    or death
Fire risk: Dangerous when exposed to heat or flames

METHYL BENZENE
(see Toluol)

METHYL CARBINOL
(see Ethanol)

METHYL-ETHYL KETONE
Synonyms: 2-Butanone, MEK
Common uses: Lacquer, wood filler, plastic cement
Toxicity (TLV in ppm): 200
Dangers: Can affect skin, central nervous system, upper respiratory tract
Fire risk: A dangerous fire and explosive hazard

METHYL-ISOBUTYL KETONE
Synonyms: Hexone, Isobutyl methyl ketone, MIBK
Common uses: Lacquer, paint, plastic cement, spray can products, varnish, wood
    filler

Toxicity (TLV in ppm): 50
Dangers: Can affect respiratory system, eyes, skin, central nervous system
Fire risk: Dangerous when exposed to heat, flame or oxidizers

METHYL N-BUTYL KETONE
Synonyms: Butyl methyl ketone, 2-hexanone, MBK
Common uses: Aerosols, lacquer, oils, quick-drying finishes, wax, varnish, wood
    filler
Toxicity (TLV in ppm): 5
Dangers: Can affect respiratory system, eyes, skin, nose, central nervous system
Fire risk: Dangerous when exposed to heat or flame

METHYLENE CHLORIDE
Synonyms: Dichloromethane, methylene dichloride
Common uses: Adhesives, contact cement, paint strippers
Toxicity (TLV in ppm): 50
Dangers: Can affect skin, kidneys, liver, central nervous system

METHYLENE DICHLORIDE
(see Methylene chloride)

MIBK
(see Methyl-isobutyl ketone)

MINERAL SPIRITS
Synonyms: Odorless paint thinner, Stoddard solvent, turpentine substitute, white
    spirits
Common uses: Varnish, polyurethane, tung oil, brush cleaner, thinner, degreaser
Toxicity (TLV in ppm): 200
Dangers: Can affect skin, lungs, central nervous system

ODORLESS PAINT THINNER
(see Mineral spirits)

PETROLEUM ETHER
(see Petroleum naphtha)

PETROLEUM NAPHTHA
Synonyms: Petroleum ether, petroleum spirits
Common uses: Lacquer, wax, paint, varnish, wood filler
Toxicity (TLV in ppm): 100
Dangers: Eyes, skin, respiratory system, central nervous system
Fire risk: Very dangerous when exposed to heat or flame

PETROLEUM SPIRITS
(see Petroleum naphtha)

PROPANONE
(see Acetone)

PYROACETIC ETHER
(see Acetone)

SPIRITS OF TURPENTINE
(see Turpentine)

STODDARD SOLVENT
(see Mineral spirits)

TOLUEN
(see Toluol)

TOLUENE
(see Toluol)

TOLUOL

Synonyms: Methyl benzene, toluen, toluene, toluolo
Common uses: Adhesives, lacquer thinner, finishing oils, polyurethane, paint stripper, wood putty
Toxicity (TLV in ppm): 100
Dangers: Eyes, skin, upper respiratory tract, central nervous system, liver, kidneys
Fire risk: Dangerous when exposed to heat or flames

TOLUOLO

(see Toluol)

TURPENTINE

Synonyms: Gum spirits, gum turpentine, spirits of turpentine, wood turpentine
Common uses: Tung oil, wax, brush cleaner, degreaser, thinner
Toxicity (TLV in ppm): 100
Dangers: Can affect skin, eyes, lungs, central nervous system, bladder, kidneys
Fire risk: Dangerous when exposed to heat, flames and oxidizers

TURPENTINE SUBSTITUTE

(see Mineral spirits)

VARNISH MAKER'S AND PAINTER'S NAPHTHA

(see VM&P naphtha)

VM&P NAPHTHA

Synonym: Varnish maker's and painter's naphtha
Common uses: Degreaser, lacquer, solvent, varnish
Toxicity (TLV in ppm): 300
Dangers: Can affect eyes, skin, lungs, central nervous system
Fire risk: Dangerous when exposed to heat, flame and oxidizers

WHITE SPIRITS

(see Mineral spirits)

WOOD ALCOHOL
(see Ethanol)

WOOD TURPENTINE
(see Turpentine)

XILOLI
(see Xylene)

XYLENE
Synonyms: Dimethyl benzene, ksylen, xilole, xyloli
Common uses: Adhesives, lacquer, paint, paint stripper
Toxicity (TLV in ppm): 100
Dangers: Can affect skin, upper respiratory tract, central nervous system
Fire risk: Dangerous fire hazard from heat, flame and powerful oxidizers

XYLOLE
(see Xylene)

CHAPTER 11

SOURCES OF SUPPLY

HARD-TO-FIND WOODWORKING SUPPLIES

Adams Wood Products
974 Forest Drive
Morristown, TN 37814
(table legs, bed posts, furniture components)

The Bartley Collection
29060 Airpark Drive
Easton, MD 21601
(antique reproduction furniture kits)

Certainly Wood
11753 Big Tree Road
East Aurora, NY 14052
(veneer)

Cherry Tree Toys
P.O. Box 369
Belmont, OH 43718
(toy plans, parts and supplies)

Christian J. Hummul Co.
404 Brooklets Avenue
Easton, MD 21601
(solid brass and solid copper sheet stock)

Country Accents
P.O. Box 437
Montoursville, PA 17754
(pierced tin, pierced copper and pierced brass)

Delta Machinery Co.
Attn: Parts Department
4290 East Raines Road
Memphis, TN 38118
Parts Department Tel. (800) 223-7278
(parts for Walker-Turner machinery)

Eagle America
P.O. Box 1099
Chardon, OH 44024
(large selection of router bits)

Floral Glass and Mirror, Inc.
895 Motor Parkway
Hauppauge, NY 11788
(beveled glass, mirror glass)

The Gold Leaf People
3 Cross Street
Suffern, NY 10901-4610
(gold leaf)

Happy House Miniatures
130 North Mail Street
Mocksville, NC 27028
(doll house supplies)

Klingspor's
P.O. Box 3737
Hickory, NC 28603-3737
(sanding supplies)

The Luthier's Mercantile
412 Moore Lane
Hearldsburg, CA 95448
(guitar wood, rosettes, inlays, and guitarmaking tools)

Maine Coast Lumber
35 Birch Hill Road
York, ME 03909
(hardwood plywood)

McFeely's
1620 Wythe Road
Lynchburg, VA 24506-1169
(square drive screws)

Micro-Mark
340 Snyder Avenue
Berkeley Heights, NJ 07922-1595
(thin lumber, small tools for modelmakers)

MLCS
P.O. Box 4053
Rydal, PA 19046
(large selection of router bits)

Oakwood Veneer Company
3642 West 11 Mile Road
Berkley, MI 48072
(veneer)

Ohio Tool Systems
3863 Congress Parkway
Richfield, OH 44286
(parts for Millers Falls Co. machinery)

The Old Fashioned Milk Paint Company
P.O. Box 222
Groton, MA 01450
(milk paint)

Osborne Wood Products
Highway 123 North
Route 3, Box 551
Toccoa, GA 30577
(turned table legs, bed posts)

Pearl Works
Rt. 3, Box 122
Mechanicsville, MD 20659
(mother-of-pearl inlay)

Reid Tool Supply
2265 Black Creek Road
Muskegon, MI 49444-2684
(plastic knobs and handles for jig making)

Ridge Carbide Tool Company
595 New York Avenue
Lyndhurst, NJ 07071
(custom-made router bits)

River Bend Turnings
3730 Vandermark Road
Scio, NY 14880
(custom turning)

Shaker Workshops
P.O. Box 1028
Concord, MA 07142
(chair tape for Shaker chairs)

Tremont Nail Company
8 Elm Street
Wareham, MA 02571
(old-fashioned cut nails, colonial hardware)

Veneer Products, Ltd.
1140 Bronx River Avenue
Bronx, NY 10472
(veneer)

Woodworker's Dream
10 West North Street
Nazareth, PA 18064
(thin wood)

Woodworks
4500 Anderson Boulevard
Fort Worth, TX 76117
(miscellaneous small wood parts)

Zaharoff Industries
26 Max Avenue
Hicksville, NY 11801
(mother-of-pearl inlay)

GENERAL WOODWORKING SUPPLIERS

Constantine's
2050 Eastchester Road
Bronx, NY 10461

Craftsman Wood Service
1735 West Cortland Court
Addison, IL 60101-4280

Frog Tool Company
700 West Jackson Boulevard
Chicago, IL 60606

Garrett Wade Company
161 Avenue of the Americas
New York, NY 10013

Highland Hardware
1045 N. Highland Ave., N.E.
Atlanta, GA 30306

Seven Corners Ace Hardware
216 West 7th Street
St. Paul, MN 55102

Shopsmith, Inc.
3931 Image Drive
Dayton, OH 45414-2591

Trend-Lines
375 Beacham Street
Chelsea, MA 02150

Woodcraft Supply Corporation
210 Wood County Industrial Park
Parkersburg, WV 26102

Woodworker's Supply
5604 Alameda, N.E.
Albuquerque, NM 87113

HARDWARE SUPPLIERS

Anglo-American Brass Company
Box 9487
San Jose, CA 95157

Ball and Ball
463 West Lincoln Highway
Exton, PA 19341

Classic Hardware
Garrett Wade Company
161 Avenue of the Americas
New York, NY 10013

Horton Brasses
P.O. Box 120
Cromwell, CT 06416

Imported European Hardware
5461 South Arville
Las Vegas, NV 89118

Meisel Hardware Specialties
P.O. Box 70
Mound, MN 55364-0070

Paxton Hardware, Ltd.
P.O. Box 256
Upper Falls, MD 21156

Period Furniture Hardware Company
Box 314, Charles Street Station
Boston, MA 02114

Rufkahrs
4207 Eaglerock Court
St. Charles, MO 63304

Stanley Hardware
195 Lake Street
New Britain, CT 06050

Whitechapel, Ltd.
Box 136
3650 West Highway 22
Wilson, WY 83014

The Wise Company
6503 St. Claude
Arabi, LA 70032

HARDWOOD SUPPLIERS

American Woodcrafters
905 South Roosevelt Avenue
Piqua, OH 45356

Arroyo Hardwoods
2585 Nina Street
Pasadena, CA 91107

Austin Hardwoods
2119 Goodrich
Austin, TX 78704

Berea Hardwoods Company
125 Jacqueline Drive
Berea, OH 44017

Bergers Hardwoods
Route 4, Box 195
Bedford, VA 24523

Berkshire Products
Route 7A
Sheffield, MA 01257

Bristol Valley Hardwoods
4054 Route 64
Canandaigua, NY 14424

Maurice L. Condon
248 Ferris Avenue
White Plains, NY 10603

Craftwoods
10921-L York Road
Hunt Valley, MD 21030

Croffwood Mills
RD #1, Box 14J
Driftwood, PA 15832

Croy-Marietta Hardwoods, Inc.
121 Pike Street, Box 643
Marietta, OH 45750

Dimension Hardwoods, Inc.
113 Canal Street
Shelton, CT 06484

Dunham Hardwoods
R.R. 1, Box 126
Dunlap, IA 51529

Educational Lumber Company
P.O. Box 5373
Asheville, NC 28813

Exotic Hardwoods and Veneers
1154 57th Avenue
Oakland, CA 94621

Garreson Lumber
RD 3
Bath, NY 14810

General Woodcraft
531 Broad Street
New London, CT 06320

Gilmer Wood Company
2211 N.W. St. Helens Road
Portland, OR 97210

Goby Walnut Products
5016 Palestine Road
Albany, OR 97321

Groff & Hearne Lumber, Inc.
858 Scotland Road
Quarryville, PA 17566

Hardwoods of Memphis
P.O. Box 12449
Memphis, TN 38182-0449

Hennegan's Wood Shed
7760 Southern Boulevard
West Palm Beach, FL 33411

Kaymar Wood Products
4603 35th S.W.
Seattle, WA 98126

Kountry Kraft Hardwoods
R.R. No. 1
Lake City, IA 51449

Leonard Lumber Company
P.O. Box 2396
Brandford, CT 06405

MacBeath Hardwood Company
930 Ashby Avenue
Berkeley, CA 94710

McFeely's Hardwoods and Lumber
P.O. Box 3
712 12th Street
Lynchburg, VA 24505

Native American Hardwoods
Route 1
West Valley, NY 14171

Niagra Lumber
47 Elm Street
East Aurora, NY 14052

Northend Hardwoods
Red Village Road
Lyndonville, VT 05851

Northland Forest Products
Depot Road
Kingston, NH 03848

Sterling Hardwoods, Inc.
412 Pine Street
Burlington, VT 05401

Steve Wall Lumber Company
Box 287
Mayodan, NC 27027

Talarico Hardwoods
RD 3, Box 3268
Mohnton, PA 19540

Wood World
1719 Chestnut
Glenview, IL 60025

Woodcrafter's Supply
7703 Perry Highway (Rt. 19)
Pittsburgh, PA 15237

Wood-Ply Lumber Corporation
100 Benington Avenue
Freeport, NY 11520

Woodworker's Dream
P.O. Box 329
Nazareth, PA 18064

Woodworker's Source
5402 South 40th Street
Phoenix, AZ 85040

WOOD FINISHING SUPPLIERS

Finishing Products and Supply Company
4611 Macklind Avenue
St. Louis, MO 63109

Hood Finishing Products, Inc.
P.O. Box 220
Tennent, NJ 07763-0220

Industrial Finishing Products
465 Logan Street
Brooklyn, NY 11208

The Wise Company
6503 St. Claude
Arabi, LA 70032

Wood Finishing Enterprises
1729 North 68th Street
Wauwatosa, WI 53212

Wood Finishing Supply Company
100 Throop Street
Palmyra, NY 14522

CLOCK PARTS SUPPLIERS

The American Clockmaker
P.O. Box 326
Clintonville, WI 54929

Armor Products
P.O. Box 445
East Northport, NY 11731

Klockit, Inc.
P.O. Box 542
Lake Geneva, WI 53147

S. LaRose
234 Commerce Place
Greensboro, NC 27420

Newport Enterprises
2313 West Burbank Boulevard
Burbank, CA 91506

Turncraft Clocks, Inc.
P.O. Box 100
Mound, MN 55364-0100

COMPREHENSIVE INDEX

Drying time for lumber, 97-99
Drywall screws, 154

E

Edge miter joints, 40
Ellipse, 17-18
End lap joints, 40
End miter joints, 40
Epoxy, 122-125
Equilibrium moisture content for woods,
    90-92
Examples. *See also* Woodshop Applications
    grid patterns, enlarging with photocopy
        machine, 35-37
    particleboard shelf loads, 57
    polygons, determining side lengths, 32
Exposure durability, of manufactured woods,
    106
Extension cord lengths, 181

F

Fasteners, 151-166
    brads, 163
    butt hinges, 164
    carriage bolts, 162
    dowel screws, 160
    drywall screws, 154
    hanger bolts, 159
    hinges, butt, 164
    lag screws, 160-161
    machine bolts, 158
    machine screws, 158
    machine threads, standard, 157
    MDF screws, 154
    nails, 155-156
    particleboard screws, 154
    rosan nuts, 165
    screws. *See specific screw*
    sheetrock screws, 154
    tee-nuts, 166
    threaded inserts, 165
    washers, 163
    wood screws, 152-153
Fiberboard, medium density (MDF).
    See Medium density fiberboard
    (MDF)
Finger joints, 42
Finishing, 167-177
    coated abrasives, 168-173. *See also* Coated
      abrasives
    Danish oil, 176-177
    lacquer, 176-177
    polyurethane, 176-177

shellac, 174, 176-177
    stains, 175
    steel wool, 173
    tack rags, 177
    topcoats, 176-177. *See also* Topcoats
    tung oil, 176-177
    varnish, 176-177
Flat miter joints, 40
Floor molding, 59
Forstner drill bits, 128
Fractions to decimal equivalents, 19
Fractions to metric equivalents, 20
Full round molding, 59
Furniture design, 38-66
    abbreviations, woodworking, 54-55
    acrylic sheet, 66
    beds, 50
    chairs, 46
    desks, 49
    dimensions, 46-52. *See also specific piece of*
      furniture
    joinery. *See specific joints*
    kitchen cabinets, 52
    molding, 59-62. *See also specific molding*
    particleboard shelf loads, 56-58
    pilot hole drill size, 63-65
    plastic laminate, 66
    screw shank size, 63-65
    shelves, 51
    shop drawings, 53-54
    symbols, woodworking, 56
    tables, 47-48
    workbenches, 51

G

Geometry, 2-18
    angles, 2, 33-35
    area formulas, 7-9
    circles, 6, 37
    circumference formula, 12
    compound angles, 33-35
    ellipse, 17-18
    perimeter formulas, 10-11
    polygons, 3, 5, 30-32
    quadrilaterals, 4
    triangles, 3, 13-16
Glue. *See* Adhesives
Grades of woods, 77-87, 106-108, 111-115.
    See also Woods, generally
Grid patterns, enlarging with photocopy
    machine, 35-37
Groove joints, 39

nose and cove, 60
panel, 62
picture, 60
quarter round, 61
sanitary stop, 61
screen, 62
shoe, 59
solid crown, 60
square block, 59
Molding head cutters, 138-139
Mortise and tenon joints, 41-42
blind, 41
haunched, 41
open, 42
pinned, 42
round, 41
stub, 41
through, 41

N

Nail joints, 45
Nails, 155-156
Neck molding, 59
Noise exposure and levels, 182-183
Nose and cove molding, 60

O

Open mortise and tenon joints, 42

P

Panel molding, 62
Particleboard, 117
screws, 154
shelf loads, 56-58
Perimeter formulas, 10-11
Photocopy machine, enlarging grid patterns
using, 35-37
Picture molding, 60
Pilot hole drill size, 63-65
Pinned mortise and tenon joints, 42
Plane irons, sharpening, 146
Plastic laminate, 66
Plywood, 104-116
core construction, 113
exposure durability, 106
grades, 106-108, 111-115
matching, 114
softwood, 104-108
span ratings, 107
species category, 110
species group number, 105
standard thickness, 104-108, 109
veneer grade, 106

Polygons, 3, 5, 30-32
side lengths, determining, 32
Polyurethane, 122-125, 176-177
Polyvinyl acetate, 122-125
Pressure-treated lumber, 85-87
safety, 184
Pulleys, 135

Q

Quadrilaterals, 4
Quarter round molding, 61

R

Rabbet joints, 39
Rabbet miter joints, 40
Radial saw blades, 140-141
Resorcinol, 122-125
Rosan nuts, 165
Round mortise and tenon joints, 41
Routers, 136-137

S

Saber saws, 134
Safety, 178-193
extension cord lengths, 181
general rules, 179-180
hazardous chemicals, 185-193
noise exposure and levels, 182-183
pressure-treated wood, 184
Sandpaper. *See* Coated abrasives, generally
Sanitary stop molding, 61
Screen molding, 62
Screw joints, 45
Screws
dowel, 160
drywall, 154
lag, 160-161
machine, 158
machine threads, standard, 157
particleboard, 154
sheetrock, 154
wood, 152-153
Screw shank size, 63-65
Scroll saws, 132-133
Sharpening, 145-150
carving gouges, 147
chisels, 146
drawknives, 147
jointer blades, 147
plane irons, 146
spokeshaves, 146
stones, 149-150
turning chisels, 148

MORE GREAT BOOKS
FOR YOUR WOODSHOP!

Creating Beautiful Boxes With Inlay Techniques—Now building elegant boxes is easy with this handy reference featuring 13 full-color, step-by-step projects! Thorough directions and precise drawings will have you creating beautiful inlaid boxes with features ranging from handcut dovetails to hidden compartments.
#70368/$24.99/128 pages/230 color, 30 b&w illus./paperback

Build Your Own Kitchen Cabinets—Build beautiful, sturdy kitchen cabinets, no matter what your skill level! Step-by-step directions walk you through planning, design, construction and installation. And a range of cabinetry designs will ensure that the cabinets you build are the right ones for you!
#70376/$22.99/136 pages/170 + b&w illus./paperback

Mastering Hand Tool Techniques—Get the most from your hand tools! Over 180 tools are detailed with step-by-step instructions on how to use and care for them properly. Plus, you'll make the most of your work with tips on wood selection, precise measuring and flawless sawing, turning, carving and joinery.
#70364/$27.99/144 pages/300 + color illus.

Earn a Second Income From Your Woodworking—Turn your hobby into income with the stories of 15 professional woodworkers and the secrets they used to make their dream come true! You'll get the inside story on business planning, marketing, workshop design and tax issues to help you make the most of your dreams, too!
#70377/$22.99/128 pages/42 b&w illus./paperback

Build Your Own Router Tables—Increase your router's accuracy, versatility and usefulness with a winning table design. Detailed plans and instructions for 3 types of tables plus a variety of specialty jigs and fixtures will help you create the right table for your shop. *#70367/$21.99/160 pages/300 illus./paperback*

The Encyclopedia of Joint Making—Create the best joints for every project! This comprehensive resource shows you how to prepare lumber, prevent layout errors, select the right joint, choose the best fastener and more.
#70356/$22.99/144 pages/300+ color illus.

The Woodworker's Guide to Furniture Design—Discover what it takes to design visually pleasing and comfortably functional furniture. Garth Graves shows you how to blend aesthetics and function with construction methods and material characteristics to develop designs that really work! *#70355/$27.99/208 pages/110 illus.*

Build Your Own Entertainment Centers—Now you can customize the construction and design of an entertainment center to fit your skill level, tools, style and budget. With this heavily illustrated guidebook, you'll explore the whole process—from selecting the wood to hardware and finishing. *#70354/$22.99/128 pages/paperback*

Good Wood Finishes—Take the mystery out of one of woodworking's most feared tasks! With detailed instructions and illustrations you'll learn about applying the perfect finish, preparing materials, repairing aged finishes, graining wood and much more.
#70343/$19.99/128 pages/325+ color illus.

Measure Twice, Cut Once, Revised Edition—Miscalculation will be a thing of the past when you learn these effective techniques for checking and adjusting measuring tools, laying out complex measurements, fixing mistakes, making templates and much more! #70330/$22.99/144 pages/144 color illus.

100 Keys to Woodshop Safety—Make your shop safer than ever with this manual designed to help you avoid potential pitfalls. Tips and illustrations demonstrate the basics of safe shopwork—from using electricity safely and avoiding trouble with hand and power tools to ridding your shop of dangerous debris and handling finishing materials. #70333/$17.99/64 pages/125 color illus./paperback

Making Elegant Gifts From Wood—Develop your woodworking skills and make over 30 gift-quality projects at the same time! You'll find everything you're looking to create in your gifts—variety, timeless styles, pleasing proportions and imaginative designs that call for the best woods. Plus, technique sidebars and hardware installation tips make your job even easier. #70331/$24.99/128 pages/30 color, 120 b&w illus.

Getting the Very Best From Your Router—Get to know your router inside and out as you discover new jigs and fixtures to amplify its capabilities, as well as techniques to make it the most precise cutting tool in your shop. Plus, tips for comparing different routers and bits will help you buy smart for a solid, long-term investment. #70328/$22.99/144 pages/225+ b&w illus.

Good Wood Handbook, 2nd Edition—Now you can select and use the right wood for the job—before you buy. You'll discover valuable information on a wide selection of commercial softwoods and hardwoods—from common uses, color and grain to how the wood glues and takes finish. #70329/$19.99/128 pages/250 color illus.

100 Keys to Preventing & Fixing Woodworking Mistakes—Stop those mistakes before they happen—and fix those that have already occurred. Numbered tips and color illustrations show you how to work around flaws in wood; fix mistakes made with the saw, plane, router and lathe; repair badly made joints, veneering mishaps and finishing blunders; assemble projects successfully and more! #70332/$17.99/64 pages/125 color illus.